Advance praise for
Leading for a Change

"I have been reading about leadership for forty years, and most of what I have read is just pabulum. This is not that."
—**Beverly Brumbaugh,** Vice President,
Human Resources and Corporate Excellence,
Sheldahl Corporation

"In his book, Ralph Jacobson provides excellent practical and insightful advice through situational examples on how to 'lead change'. Secondly, he provides useful tools for leaders to assess their own leadership capabilities and become more successful. This is an invaluable resource for any leader interested in leading change."
—**S. Tyrone Alexander,** Senior Vice President,
Human and Administrative Services,
HighMark BlueCross BlueShield

"Mr. Jacobson makes a contribution to change leaders by providing an easy-to-understand 'Leader's Map' and, most importantly, the practical tools and applicable how-to's to go along with it. While pushing the edges with new information, he also offers solid, time-tested foundational concepts and approaches to help leaders take action."
—**Kate O'Keefe,** Director of Executive Education
and Development, Honeywell

"The Leader's Map elegantly captures the essence of leadership. Not only is it applicable in the digital age, this model will transcend through time."
—**Rajeev Peshawaria**, Director,
Global Learning & Performance, American Express

"*Leading for a Change* should be the official operator's manual for anyone sitting in the president's chair. It cuts through the management theories and targets the heart of the everyday challenges faced by leaders. Real world examples make *Leading for a Change* a treasure trove for top executives. Leading an organization through growth and change is a far less risky proposition after reading this book."
—**Nick Bruyer,** President, Asset Marketing Services, Inc.

"Are leaders born or can leadership be learned? My answer is *both* of the above. Having already been born...your only remaining opportunity to enhance your leadership skills is to learn and practice your learnings.

Leading for a Change clearly maps out a pragmatic and demonstrated 'real world' leadership process. I believe that by focusing on the few fundamental leadership tasks outlined in this book you can move your business/organization significantly forward."

—**Dr. James Behnke,** Advisor to the CEO,
The Pillsbury Company

"Most popular books on leadership are entertaining but soon forgotten. Here's an interesting book you can actually do something with: a step-by-step action plan to becoming a more effective leader from one of the better 'out-of-the-box' thinkers I've met."

—**Jim Hartman,** CEO & President, MedAmicus, Inc.

"Ralph Jacobson has captured what it truly means to be a great leader. This book stands out as a practical, solutions-oriented guide to becoming an effective leader. It provides the necessary framework, real life examples of leadership, tips, and step-by-step approaches that are essential in building leadership skills."

—**Louis L. Carter,** Manager of Publications/Consultant,
Linkage, Inc.

"In a world of books on leadership, this one stands out as a sound, practical guide. Ralph Jacobson has captured what it means to be a leader in the 21st century."

—**Daniel S. Hanson,** President, Fluid Dairy Division of
Land O'Lakes, Inc.; author, *A Place to Shine: Emerging from
the Shadows at Work and Cultivating Common Ground:
Releasing the Power of Relationships at Work*

"*Leading for a Change* succinctly reveals what leaders should do to achieve financial and business objectives. It adeptly elucidates how leaders can engage employees to build more productive and agile organizations. It is eminently practical; it does an exemplary job of streamlining the learning required to be a leader."

—**Dr. David Owens,** Chief Knowledge Officer
& Vice President of Learning & Development,
The Saint Paul Companies

LEADING FOR A CHANGE

May the map & tools take your leadership to a new level.

Ralph

LEADING FOR A CHANGE

How to Master the 5 Challenges
Faced by Every Leader

by

RALPH JACOBSON

with

Keith Setterholm
John Vollum

Boston   Oxford   Auckland   Johannesburg   Melbourne   New Delhi

Butterworth Heinemann is an imprint of Elsevier.

∞ This book is printed on acid-free paper.

Library of Congress Cataloging-in-Publication Data
Jacobson, Ralph, 1948-
    Leading for a change : How to master the 5 challenges faced by every leader / by Ralph Jacobson with Keith Setterholm, John Vollum.
    p.   cm.
 Includes bibliographical references.
    ISBN 0-7506-7279-X (pbk. : alk.paper)
        1. Leadership. 2. Executive ability. I. Setterholm, Keith
        II.   Vollum, John.   III. Title.
HD57.7 J337 2000
658.4'092—dc21

                                        00-024632

British Library Cataloguing-in-Publication Data
A catalogue record for this book is available from the British Library.

The publisher offers special discounts on bulk orders of this book.
For information, please contact:
Manager of Special Sales
Elsevier
200 Wheeler Road
Burlington, MA 01803
Tel: 781-313-4700
Fax: 781-313-4802

For information on all Butterworth-Heinemann publications available, contact our World Wide Web homepage at http://www.bhusa.com/

10 9 8 7 6 5 4 3 2
Printed in the United States of America.

To Carrie,
who was always there . . . every step of the way

Contents

About Synthesis

People are an organization's most critical and expensive resource. Managed effectively, they are a powerful force to leverage against the competition and sustain long-term organizational health. Leadership is the catalyst that creates a cohesive and vibrant workforce. But the rate of change and its resulting stress reduce the time people have to develop their leadership skills. Just when more leadership is required, we typically find it in short supply.

Synthesis is forging a new paradigm for enhancing leadership. We believe in the following principles:

- Leadership need not be a solo act. Leaders support each other to accomplish organizational objectives.
- Leadership can be learned, thus it is less art and mostly practice.
- Leadership that consistently uses proven processes is more likely to achieve its objectives.
- The most successful leaders focus on using their strengths effectively.
- Effective leaders learn to use leadership tools in ways that are natural to them.

To learn more about Synthesis and our approach to leadership development, visit our website at www.leadingforachange.com. There you will find additional resources, leadership tools, and further information about our organization. We are also interested in learning about new tools and helping you with your journey.

 **Synthesis**

7801 East Bush Lake Road
Suite 360
Minneapolis, MN 55439
952-831-7488

Preface

As a Human Resources executive, consultant, and executive coach, I have been blessed with close relationships with many leaders. I have watched intelligent, capable, and caring people struggle to connect with their employees. I have seen well-crafted plans fall deafly on the ears of cynical employees. Too often leaders return from leadership development programs eager to create a new reality and are unable to find the peer support to do so. Many leaders I have worked with sincerely wanted to engage their employees in new ways. They understood the limitations of the traditional command and control model. Yet, the purest of intentions were often met with resistance. Surprised, confused, and disappointed, the leaders often retreated to the more familiar leader/subordinate role.

We have reengineered, teamed, flattened, and automated. Yet all of this remains insufficient. The widespread dissatisfaction of employees with their leadership and the increased stress felt by the leaders themselves suggest that a new paradigm of leadership is in order. We need to realize that no one person possesses all the talents to run an organization over the long term. Instead, we must see "leader" as a person and "leadership" as a critical organization function. Leadership does not have to be a solo act. People with complementary skills who learn to function as a leadership team are more likely to build long-term organization success. We have expected employees on the shop floor to work together. Now we expect our leaders to do so. Contrary to popular opinion, I believe the problem of leadership lies less often with the individuals, and more with the inability of the traditional structure, process, and expectations.

People who want to share leadership responsibilities and tap the talent around them need new ways of working together. They need to establish a common understanding of what will be delivered, how they can more effectively work together, and how they will assess their leadership performance. Thus, we need to find ways to help leaders work together more productively.

Leaders have enough theory. *Leading for a Change* prescribes what leaders can do to ensure the success of their organizations. It integrates proven best practices into an easy-to-use manual that helps leaders know what to do when and how to accomplish it. The Leader's Map in Chapter 1 provides a framework that enables leaders to see both the order and rhythm to their work. The language and the picture of the model create the possibilities for leaders to better understand their responsibilities and also establish the framework for a group of leaders to work together to meet the leadership challenges of the organization. The tools described in the subsequent chapters encourage leaders to include a larger number of people to come together and establish the agenda for the organization. The map and tools provide the means to find a leadership balance to both maintain control and also invite others to participate in setting the agenda and resolving the difficulties typically encountered in organizational life.

The first chapter provides the overview and foundation for a new way to look at leadership. It describes five universally experienced leadership challenges. The remaining chapters provide explicit steps leaders can take to address the challenges. Readers are encouraged not to read the book from cover to cover, but to focus on those chapters that are of greatest interest to them. The process and tools are useful for an organization's chief executive, the leadership group, the manager who wants to be a leader, and the leader's coach. Human Resources professionals responsible for developing the leadership talent will find this book to be a helpful foundation upon which to build a program for managers to become leaders.

The examples interwoven within the chapters are the stories of leaders who were committed to finding a better way. I owe these people, my clients, a special word of thanks for allowing me into their lives and providing an opportunity to collaborate and learn from each other.

Deane Gradous continues to be a valued friend. Her encouragement to pursue my dream and her editorial assistance and persistence deserve special thanks.

Most of all, I owe gratitude and thanks to my wife Carrie, who saw this book many years before I did. Thank you for creating the space and providing the support to make it possible.

Ralph Jacobson

Introduction

Once they work with Jim, people easily see why he has successfully taken his company from $5 to $45 million in revenues in a matter of a few years. He has an excellent grasp of the needs of his customers, he knows how to build strategic relationships, and his marketing skills are unparalleled. Employees recognize that without Jim there would be no company.

Yet the company is in grave danger, perhaps on the verge of extinction. A recent layoff reduced the number of employees by 15 percent. The sales force has fallen far short of its projected sales, employees are less able to work together, and morale is suffering. Jim is frustrated because he believes in a potential for huge success. He anticipates a very bright future, but he also feels burdened with getting through the company's current problems.

Although he possesses excellent business skills, Jim is not prepared to take on the leadership challenges that lie before him. He has had few role models. A liberal arts education and a limited study of finance have not prepared him to lead. And the board of directors wants answers, not questions. Employees, shareholders, suppliers, bankers, and customers want a confident leader, one who can point the way to success. They are not interested in following a leader who has more questions than answers.

Publicly, Jim expresses a positive attitude. To his wife and his closest friends, however, Jim candidly expresses his concerns. He questions the capabilities of his direct reports; he wonders how long funds to run the company will be available. He doesn't know whom he can trust, and most important, he doesn't know if he can move the company forward. He has always been able to get out of difficult situations. He has always talked his way out of tight corners. He now painfully realizes that the skills that once worked so brilliantly will no longer suffice to overcome the challenges before him.

Jim is not unusual. At some point in our careers, most of us learn that what we know is not enough, that what worked before no longer does. We discover a need for new approaches, tools, and skills. Those of us who survive this leadership challenge usually find ourselves stronger as a result. When we feel unable to meet this challenge, we yearn for more sophisticated advice, a different course of action, or a better understanding of our options.

It is part of the natural life cycle to be confronted with challenges and to learn how to solve them so we can take on the next issue. But the truth is that being in charge of an organization that is constantly under fire or having to adapt can be painful. We find leadership to be a lonely and frustrating role. Few share our zeal or our view of the company. If only we could solve the people problems!

Ironically, leadership has been the subject of hundreds of authors for thousands of years. Today, books on leadership rank high on the nation's list of bestsellers. How can it be that so well scrutinized a subject remains a mystery? How can it be that when we need advice the most it seems to be the least accessible?

This book can be of help to you. It is not a book on "leadership made easy." There is no such possibility. This is not a book on "follow these three easy steps." This is a book that synthesizes the best approaches of many thinkers to form a systematic model for looking at the job. The Leader's Map will help you gain a clearer understanding of your role, which is to get people excited about working for your company, to figure out how to make the right things happen, and ultimately to achieve the results you and your associates are looking for. Although the leadership role can be lonely, it can also be exciting. Although the fear of failure can be haunting, making things happen can be exhilarating. Improving your leadership skills will not only be of value to your career; it will also be of great benefit to those who work for you or with you.

What Do Leaders Do?

Jim is a very busy person. Although leadership of the company was an important issue, a number of weeks went by before he found the time to visit with a management consultant. After an initial exchange of pleasantries, the consultant began to explore the realities of Jim's leadership activities. He asked Jim to describe his role. Jim easily developed a list of activities and projects. He said he communicated regularly with the financial community to raise money for a new building. He had recently intervened with two of his direct reports who were not getting along. A number of product problems required his immediate attention. And he normally spent an inordinate amount of time with customers to ensure that the sales goals for the month would be achieved.

After listing his activities, Jim sat back in his chair. He realized why he was feeling so stressed and fatigued. He expected the consultant to commiserate. But sympathy was not forthcoming.

The consultant was not being insensitive. Rather, he realized that Jim was caught in a struggle between being actively involved in the nitty-gritty details of the business and trying to focus on the larger, longer-term needs of the business. Jim felt that by focusing his efforts on quarterly, bottom-line objectives, he was doing what was necessary to make the right things happen. Unfortunately, while he tended to everyday needs, Jim unconsciously jeopardized the long-term health of the organization.

The consultant insisted that Jim further define his role. At this point, Jim quoted something he had read in a book about mission, vision, and values. The consultant asked him to describe how these things were being developed and used in his organization. Jim was unable to answer the question because he strongly believed these things would provide little value. Rather, his job was to satisfy the demands of the board of directors. The consultant asked him to describe his relationship with the board. It soon became clear this relationship, too, was strained. Jim thought it important to keep the board at arm's length.

On a typical day, Jim moved from problem to problem. At the end of the day he was exhausted and deeply dissatisfied, knowing that he had fallen far short of making the impact he had intended. He knew that what he had accomplished was insufficient to enable his company to reach even its most critical objectives. There must be more to leadership, he thought, but he did not have the "luxury" of time to find out. Now that the situation in his organization had deteriorated, he was ready to ask for advice.

Jim half expected the consultant to provide a silver bullet that would fix the company's problems. Both of them knew it was unrealistic. But it was a tempting thought. For Jim, an outsider's advice could be the means to reduce the anxiety he experienced, and the consultant would have the satisfaction of solving an important dilemma. However, rather than trying to fix immediate problems, the consultant realized that it would be more helpful to provide Jim with a new view of his role in the company. Rather than responding to the stack of issues on Jim's plate, it would be more helpful to reflect on what the organization needed at this time. Both agreed that the consultant's role was not to resolve immediate issues, but to enable Jim to redefine his leadership role and to learn to apply people and other resources more creatively.

Reality Check

Perhaps you see a little of Jim's situation in your own. If you do, you are typical of many leaders whose appetites for accomplishment are larger than they are able to realize. Before we describe a different way to look at Jim's job, you might find it helpful to take a personal inventory to discover how you approach your own work. This first exercise, which will take only a few minutes, can lead to important insights about your specific situation.

Step 1:

Imagine that the consultant is coming to your office. Because he arrives a few minutes early, he has time to chat with the receptionist and several other employees who are moving around the entryway. After a few minutes of idle conversation he asks them to describe you, what you do, your impact on the company, your vision for the organization, and your effectiveness. After 10 minutes of listening, what has he learned? Step into the consultant's shoes and take the time to write your answers on a sheet of paper before moving to Step 2.

Step 2:

Imagine that just as the consultant finishes hearing your employees' responses, you meet him at the reception area. You provide a

Table 1: Reality Check

Employees' Perceptions of You	Your Self- Assessment	Significant Differences? Why?	Implications?

brief tour of your facility before going to your office. After a few moments, the consultant asks you to describe your job, your vision of the organization, and your assessment of your effectiveness. Standing in your own shoes, take a few moments to write your responses in the first column of Table 1.

Step 3:
Compare the two lists. Table 1 will be helpful in developing your analysis.

Leaders Are Not Just Leaders

Most leaders, after they complete the exercise, find significant differences between how they view themselves and how others see them. Like most leaders, you may be discouraged by the disparities between your intentions and the perceptions of your employees. There are reasons for these disparities.

Unless you are the leader of a large company or division, it is likely that you are frequently called upon to simultaneously fulfill several roles:

The Individual Contributor Role

Most leaders have tasks that they are directly responsible for. They may have specific sales goals, relationships with the bank and other critical stakeholders, assignments from the board of directors, and so on. They sometimes accomplish much of this work without relying on the support of others. Most people are comfortable serving in the capacity of the individual contributor because the associated activities rely on skills they have developed over a number of years, are somewhat less complex because they involve fewer people, and typically have a tangible output. Given the choice, many leaders prefer to spend most of their time in the individual-contributor role. Accomplishing tasks that are important to the short-term success of the organization will also provide a high degree of personal satisfaction. Unfortunately, others will neither see nor appreciate these task contributions. As a result, they won't value the leader's task successes. When leaders spend too much time accomplishing tasks, they jeopardize the long-term health of the organization. They fail to provide the glue that holds the organization together.

The Manager Role

Managing is about creating predictability and order. Managers plan for performance, delegate responsibilities, allocate resources, and ensure results. Until the early 1990s, many professional people aspired to become managers for reasons of status and for the financial rewards that come with that status. Through management training, most learned how to motivate a small group of people to achieve a short-term result. They understand the need for budgets, performance reviews, job training, and so on. Managing is important because unless small steps are achieved along the way, the long-term objectives of the organization will not be achieved.

Most organizations have structures that demand management actions from their leaders. The Finance Department wants a budget, the Human Resources Department wants performance appraisals to be completed, employees want conflicts between departments to be settled, and people want problems to be solved. The combination of accomplishing tasks and meeting managerial demands can be fully time-consuming. Hardworking leaders may thus readily assume that they are fulfilling the obligations of their position. Although leaders may not be as comfortable being managers as they are being individual contributors, they do understand the importance of management. They have learned the principles, and they can implement them well.

Careful and consistent application of management principles will be helpful in the short term to establish greater predictability and to resolve specific organizational issues. However, such work is ineffective in developing an environment that encourages employees to be creative, take risks, communicate authentically, and assume responsibility for making the right things happen. Although most leaders seek to create a productive work environment, they often struggle with their inability to achieve this goal.

The Leader Role

Leadership is a process of helping individuals, departments, and organizations adapt to change. It means bringing out people's ability to collaborate. Leadership means moving the organization "out of the box" so that it is able to sustain the forces of change that challenge its long-term existence. Leadership is a process of determining what the organization should become, and aligning the necessary people and financial resources to achieve far beyond what they now accomplish. It is about inspiring people to follow.

The responsible leader, the person with the name and title on the door, often doesn't understand how to do all these things—for good reason. Most people have not had an opportunity to work with good leaders. In most organizations there are few opportunities for leadership coaching and mentoring. Further, the new leader will typically have the unreasonable expectation that those who become leaders have a natural ability to carry out the function from their first day on the job. Although the topic of leadership has been written about for thousands of years, the skill of applying solid leadership principles throughout an organization remains somewhat of a mystery.

What Is Your Mix?

Earlier you completed the Reality Check exercise. You noted what it is that the employees think you do. We can now take this exercise a step further.

Step 1:

Categorize your activities according to the three roles of individual contributor, manager, and leader. Some may fit more than one category.

Step 2:

Determine the percent of time you spend in each of these roles and how well you believe you are fulfilling the needs of the organization.

Step 3:

Reapportion your time as you believe you should. What activities should you

Do less of?
Do more of?
Devote a similar amount of time to?

If your analysis indicates that you should be spending more time in the leadership role, this book will be an important resource for you. In Chapter 1 we introduce the five most common challenges faced by leaders, and we provide a means for you to assess your leadership capabilities. In subsequent chapters, we further define five key leadership challenges and provide tools to help you become a more successful leader.

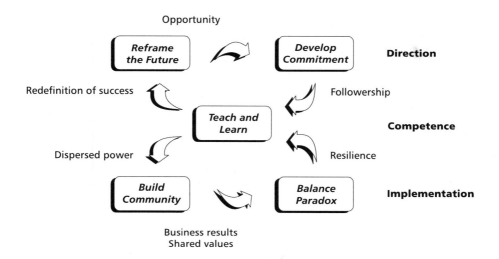

Opportunity

Reframe the Future **Develop Commitment** Direction

Redefinition of success Followership

Teach and Learn Competence

Dispersed power Resilience

Build Community **Balance Paradox** Implementation

Business results
Shared values

CHAPTER 1

The Leader's Challenges

On a Saturday morning in early fall, a small group of successful leaders gathered, not for the purpose of discussing their organizations, but to examine their roles. It soon became apparent that, although they came from different industries and with different professional preparations, they had much in common. They approached their leadership roles with a great sense of responsibility, believing that their corporation's success rested in large measure on their ability to do the job. Unfortunately, despite previous successful educational and professional experiences, they were ill prepared for the challenges that confronted them. Many struggled to define their jobs. Existing job descriptions were out of date or they listed a series of tasks that were irrelevant. Many of the leadership books they had read described what they were supposed to be, but not what they were supposed to do. In the absence of a meaningful compass, many relied on past accomplishments, hoping that what had worked in the past would once more help them succeed.

One leader synthesized five themes from the stories she had heard. As she spoke, a silence fell over the room. Every person present shared the same leadership challenges and frustrations. The most personal was also the most common. The five themes offered the leaders a way to describe their jobs in a meaningful way. They also gave the participants hope that their leadership challenges could be more adroitly addressed.

The Five Key Leadership Challenges

Whether you are a manager of a department wanting to improve service to internal customers, the project leader of a team focused on solving a thorny organizational problem, or the president of a company undertaking major change, the five challenges are important components of your leadership role. Some of these challenges may be more critical than others. Understanding the five challenges will allow you to create an agenda of what you must accomplish. Once people better understand your leadership function and your objectives, they will be more likely to follow.

1. Reframe the Future

Leaders have many opportunities to develop a broad perspective of their organizations. They understand the relationships between the dynamics in the marketplace and the dynamics in the organization. They anticipate critical changes in such areas as technology and finance, and understand the limitations of their organizations. Thus, they are able to view the business from several perspectives and can see the potential for new realities to emerge.

Reframing the future challenges leaders to develop a new set of possibilities. It provides an opportunity to rethink assumptions and relationships, and develop a new way of doing business. The result is not an operating budget for the next fiscal year, not an extension of an existing product, nor a way to reduce the cost of doing business. Reframe the future focuses on the need to refute the assumptions that bind the organization to the past. By asking the unthinkable, a leader creates the potential for a totally different kind of organization. What would happen if we partnered with our competitors? What if we used an old technology in new ways? What if we adopted a new technology to make our product or service obsolete? What if we moved from being a product manufacturer to being a service provider? What product or service would excite our customers, even make them ecstatic?

The outcome of reframing the future is your vision of a new way to add value for customers, which could enhance your organization's position in the marketplace, its productivity, or its profit picture. Your enhanced relationships with others outside the organization could lead to a significant strategic advantage. The creation of an exciting and meaningful set of possibilities is a requisite first step in developing your ability to influence change. Once the direction is established, you must convince the critical stakeholders.

2. Develop Commitment

When things go wrong in the organization, fingers point to the leaders. When things go right, fingers point to the vast majority of members of the organization. There can be no leadership without committed followers. Followers, in turn, determine that leaders will be effective. In developing commitment, leaders create clear intellectual links and active behavioral links between themselves and followers.

In our society, few people seek to be labeled as a "follower." To most people, being a follower means doing what one is told. According to our definition, followership is much more active and fulfilling. Devoted followers act with intelligence, know what to do without being told, and operate interdependently with courage and strong ethics. They distinguish when it is appropriate to follow orders, when to come back with different ideas, when to operate as individuals, and when to act as members of a unified team. In essence, they behave as if they own the business. Most leaders want such followers.

Indeed, at any particular moment a leader may recognize that an individual has a greater ability to get the job done, and assume the role of follower of that person. Thus, the leadership function may flow between people as the situation warrants.

Developing a cadre who are capable of engaging in complex relationships can be a daunting task for a leader. To become followers, people need to get something from their relationship with the leader. As Kelly notes, "Do followers, while being served, become wealthier, wiser, freer, more autonomous?"

Some followers expect perfection from their leaders. They become critical when they see weaknesses, which in turn enables them to feel less than accountable for their own performance. Better, more skilled and motivated followers understand the strengths and the weaknesses of their leaders and fill in the gap to make both parties more whole. The result is an organization with fewer hierarchical layers, a greater action orientation, and more productive dialogue. Commitment has been attained when the leader has developed a critical mass of people who are willing to address changes eagerly, honestly, and openly.

3. Teach and Learn

Teaching and learning sit at the juncture of several processes necessary to developing new concepts, developing greater competence, and implementing change. Teaching and learning is essential for organizational change to occur. They help individuals overcome the fear of taking on new challenges. They develop the competence to undertake new tasks. For these reasons, encouraging learning is a leadership function.

Progress is based on the ability of people to anticipate and plan for the future, to develop new ways of operating, to learn from each other and the past, and to implement plans swiftly and effectively. Without consciously attempting to teach and learn, people will operate as they always have. They may not be able to make the changes that will ensure their organization's long-term survival.

It is the leader's role to encourage learning throughout the organization—beginning with the leader's own learning. Effective leaders know that they cannot rely only on their innate capabilities. Rather, they hone their skills by seeking feedback, reflecting on the success of earlier actions, participating in learning forums, and surrounding themselves with those whose strengths complement their weaknesses.

Leaders ensure that sufficient competencies exist in the organization to take new ideas forward and turn them into reality. Leaders support others in seeing the world differently, in developing the competence to do their work better, in discovering how to work together more effectively, and in learning how to serve customers in ways never before imagined.

Effective teaching and learning result in your gaining new knowledge about yourself and what it is possible to accomplish.

4. Build Community

An organization requires commitment, not only from its leaders, but also from all the other members who compose it. Our focus thus far has been on the relationships between leaders and followers. Relationships that link members together in a meaningful way must also be fostered. Build Community requires leaders to consider three distinct organizational components.

Culture

Shared values provide much of the glue that holds people and their work together. Shared values can more readily be seen in the actions of employees than in the corporate handbook. Shared values indicate what people are permitted to discuss, what constitutes risk, how decisions are made, who becomes involved in making decisions, and the relative worth of stakeholder groups. Leaders who are conscious of the values they promote through their actions have a unique opportunity to influence the culture.

Infrastructure

Roads, sewers, water mains, police forces, and so on, sustain a community. Buildings, office furniture, and computer systems sustain an organization. Organization infrastructures establish the link between functions, processes, and people that ensure essential communication. Establishing firm, positive, communication links is the special responsibility of leaders. For example, leaders determine how meetings are conducted, how performance expectations are established and how performance is evaluated, how the corporate agenda is created, how teams are formed and maintained, and how everyday work is performed. Without infrastructure, leaders will have insufficient leverage to ensure that the work of the organization is communicated and performed.

Governance

Leaders clearly understand what others expect of them. They manage the expectations of key stakeholders. Leaders ensure that followers know how to measure their success, that feedback is continuously sought and given, and that reward systems are designed to recognize the desired processes and results. Leaders not only ensure performance, they also ensure that ethical practices, governmental regulations, and internal policies and procedures are enforced.

Evidence of community can be seen in the spirit and the vitality of members' relationships as they achieve the goals laid out in Reframe the Future.

5. Balance Paradox

Leaders know they have encountered a paradox when they feel as if they are "damned if they do, and damned if they don't." During the course of building community, the leader encounters reality. The real world is where critical choices must be made. Balancing paradox explains why the leadership role is often a lonely and unpopular one. The leader's and others' decisions may propel the organization to great success or bring it to its knees. In balancing paradox the true mettle of a leader is tested.

Chapter 6, "Balance Paradox," helps leaders understand how to focus on creating short-term profits while simultaneously building the capacity to compete in the long term. The leader may decide to lay off some employees and ask the remaining employees to be loyal. The leader may decide to continue a currently unprofitable core business. The leader may seek the advice of many people and yet be the only one who makes a difficult decision. The leader may not feel competent to act and yet may know that the opportunity of the moment will be lost if no action is taken.

Traditional problem-solving methods are inadequate for handling paradoxes. Professional training is also typically inadequate. Successful leaders learn to cope with paradox by rising to higher, more balanced views of situations.

The Leader's Map

Together, these five key challenges represent the heart of the leader's role. They represent what to think about as you strive to affect your organization. They are not five separate and independent challenges; all exist in a fluid interrelationship that will guide your work. These relationships are depicted in the Leader's Map in Figure 1-1.

Leaders know that much is expected of them. At any time they may analyze, define, and imagine possibilities; determine hard realities; sell, tell, and gain consensus; anticipate; demand

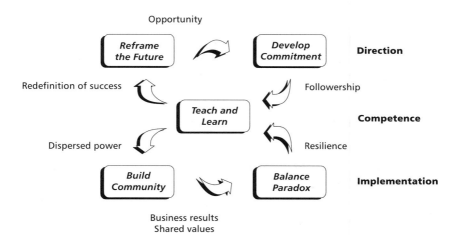

Figure 1-1: The Leader's Map

perfection or be understanding; receive feedback and give feedback; be courageous; be authentic; be out front, but not too far out front; and follow the rules or go around them. A very confusing job description!

There are appropriate times for each of these leadership behaviors. Knowing what to do when is not obvious. Just as the navigator on a ship uses a sextant to determine its position so that alterations in speed, sail, and rudder can be correctly made, so leaders use tools to determine their positions and identify necessary courses of action. The Leader's Map is a sextant, a tool for understanding the need to implement a change or take a new course. Using the Leader's Map ensures that the leader does not overemphasize one challenge at the expense of the others. Using the Map helps define the broad range of required leadership actions.

For example, a leader's first exploration of opportunities is too soon to seek consensus in the organization. Those most likely to be affected may feel threatened by undefined opportunities. Once the opportunities have been defined, the leader must listen to others' concerns, for they hold nuggets of truth worth considering. There is an appropriate and an inappropriate "season" for each leadership behavior.

The Leader's Map enables you to consider a broad range of behaviors. We believe that if you know where you are on the map, you are more likely to take effective action. For example, leaders who more readily command will know when they must listen. Those who more readily seek consensus before acting will know when they must give specific direction.

Digitex: A Successful Navigation of the Leader's Map

During the late 1980s, the company that made the largest and fastest computers in the world, Digitex (fictitious name), imploded. Unable to adroitly react to the pressures of competing foreign and emerging companies, the corporation found itself financially unstable. Initially the company divested its less profitable operations and raised additional capital. These actions were insufficient to return the organization to health.

Facing Paradox

In 1990, Harry Peterson became Digitex's chief executive officer. Harry ignored his mother's advice to turn down the job, because he felt that he was the only member of the management team capable of building a bridge to the future. The path before him was laden with risk, but Peterson's father had taught him that there would be no ceremony for those who gave up.

To create a corporate future, Peterson had to simultaneously dismember that portion of the organization that did not fit AND create a new company. He had to simultaneously meet day-to-day financial obligations AND focus on building a new future. On the one hand, Peterson had to lay off over forty thousand employees; AND on the other hand, he had to convince those who remained that they were integral to success. To those who were terminated or looking in from the outside, Peterson looked ruthless. Those who remained on the inside had to be convinced that he could be trusted to be their leader. This was a very lonely time for Harry Peterson.

Reframe the Future

Peterson decided to abandon the computer hardware business. What was once a strength had become a financial burden. Peterson believed that growth and stability rested on developing long-term, continuous relationships with clients. Rather than build computers, he would use the existing relationships with clients to establish long-term service contracts with them. For example, the company had a profitable Human Resources Payroll division. Peterson invested heavily and expanded the systems capabilities to meet the needs of large organizations with geographically dispersed needs. He also took advantage of the positive relationships with senior Human Resources professionals by offering a wide range of other services for them.

Develop Commitment

Peterson focused on four principles he believed to be critical to the success of the organization: empower employees; work as a team; create diversity; and balance the needs of employees, customers, and shareholders. Consistently living these values was clearly a challenge. For example, Peterson reduced the bonus of one of his vice presidents who successfully met financial targets, but failed to meet his diversity objectives. The consistency of word and deed was critical to establishing the trust of his direct reports.

Peterson carefully surrounded himself with capable people who possessed complementary skills. He could not delegate to mediocre people. He realized that a strong cadre of leaders would be critical to his success. The group redefined what it meant to lead, and shared the responsibilities. They established a close bond with one another. This created the power base upon which to build community.

Teach and Learn

Peterson retooled to undertake the enormous task before him. He took leadership courses, sought feedback, and developed a plan for making a personal transformation. He learned to become an extravert and communicate with a broad range of people. He learned to comfortably operate within a broad range of forums.

The employees needed to upgrade their skills. Although the company was strapped for cash, Peterson invested heavily in the training of his employees. He recognized that without new knowledge, the new corporation could not be born. Most needed to relearn how to make a profit. Peterson brought in business 101 courses; he demanded that employees understand their customers and redefine how they delivered service. The employees needed to learn to work together productively.

The corporation needed to learn to develop and successfully operate a service business. For example, the organization needed to define how it could uniquely penetrate the Human Resources market. They needed to learn how to deliver consistent service, for one disgruntled customer could have significant impact on the bottom line.

Build Community

Peterson needed to create a new identity for the company. The Digitex name carried significant baggage. He changed the name to reflect the new identity that needed to be developed.

Peterson reached out to each employee. He developed a communications plan to ensure that employees understood the new direction. He evaluated success by asking employees who were riding in the elevators with him if they knew the vision, mission, and values of the company. He also worked hard to ensure that objectives were achieved, for he realized that success would spur confidence in his leadership and in fellow employees.

Peterson hired street-smart people and ensured that they found value in working together. To accomplish this, the new organization needed to become an employer of choice—a place where people wanted to work together and win. He encouraged people to "get out of themselves and begin to take responsibility for the whole." Groups of people were brought together to hold dialogues and solve problems. He encouraged others to find the proper balance between their home and work lives.

Balance a New Paradox
Today, the organization is strong and viable. Its stock has appreciated significantly. It continues to divest itself of those operations that are less profitable and do not fit with its mission. Peterson has received several national honors for his contribution to furthering diversity. Having successfully crossed the bridge, Peterson announced his intention to retire. Perhaps now the company needs a different kind of President and CEO. Peterson has successfully worked himself out of a job. His parents would be proud.

The Primary Responsibilities of Leadership

Leaders often find it difficult to describe their jobs. The Leader's Map suggests that leaders have three major responsibilities: They establish the direction of the organization, they ensure the competency to succeed in the direction, and they ensure that the results are achieved.

Establishing Direction

It is the leader's responsibility to determine and articulate a vision, to explore opportunities for strategic linkages, and to consider new products and services that could change how the organization is positioned in the marketplace. Through facilitated planning sessions, analyses of trends, conversations with knowledgeable people, reactions to current conditions, and so on, the leader begins to formulate new ideas.

Because they are human, leaders can become somewhat enamored of their initial ideas and prone to implement them based on impulse. They may view others who question the viability of their new ideas as less than enthusiastic. The Leader's Map suggests that new ideas should be shared with others, who can thoroughly explore their viability. Leaders, at the appropriate time, must uncover the potential of their ideas prior to committing significant human and financial resources to a new direction. We have often seen leaders change their minds. A new direction that was supposed to solve a problem is dropped in favor of a still newer direction. Followers who worked hard for what they had assumed to be the long-term direction of the organization may lose faith in their leaders and be less likely to put their hearts and souls into the next initiative. When leaders change their minds, faith erodes.

Having a good idea is not enough. The Leader's Map suggests that leaders must not only be certain about the course they wish to undertake, but they must also have the understanding and the support of followers, who are needed to implement the course. Thus, the leader must ensure that ideas are well articulated and well understood. As one CEO told us, "I know that employees at least understand the direction we are going when they are able to articulate our vision, mission, and major objectives in an elevator ride from the first to the fifth floor. If they can do that, I know I have done at least one thing right. Next I look into their eyes to see if they believe it."

How will you know if you have done an adequate job of articulating the direction? The following criteria will guide your evaluation. Apply the questions to a new initiative or to a program you wish to introduce. Once you have completed the list, pose similar questions to members of your management team and determine how aligned their ideas are with each other and with yours.

The Idea
- Have I explored the idea with many people? Have I carefully taken into consideration the thoughts of those who disagree with my perspective?
- Have I developed a clear understanding of the pros and cons of implementing this idea? Do I understand the risks of moving forward and of not moving forward?
- Have I played the role of devil's advocate to my own idea?
- Are the benefits of the new direction worth the risks involved?
- Is the idea "big" enough to get the organization where it needs to be?
- Have I articulated the idea in 25 words or less and can I clearly describe the benefits and the risks? Are the idea, the benefits, and the risks understood by at least the critical few?

The Follower
- Do those who might disagree with me feel that they have been heard and understood?
- Have I established sufficient understanding in those whose support is essential to turning the idea to reality?
- Are sufficient numbers of people able to communicate the message to others in the organization?
- Do we understand the risks as best we can and are we willing to move forward?

The Learning
- Have we developed several scenarios, and have we determined the likelihood of success?
- Have we done our homework to better understand the marketplace?
- Do we know what we have to do internally to make the idea succeed?
- Have we looked for others who have attempted a similar undertaking and learned why they succeeded or why they failed?
- Have I made sure that the direction in which I wish to move the organization is sound?

Do not waste human and financial resources in an effort that is unlikely to succeed. At this point in the process of change, you will have incurred relatively few sunk costs; although some disappointments or bruised egos will be on the line if you decide not to move forward. The most costly mistakes include choosing an inappropriate direction and not properly defining the scope of a project. Unless you question your ideas early and thoroughly, such mistakes will not surface until the implementation phase.

Ensuring Competence

Many leaders assume that their work is complete when a half-baked idea develops into a sound plan. The plan is clearly articulated, and the bank is impressed. Action plans have been developed, and people are expected to "turn on a dime" in order to meet the expectations of the leadership team. If the plan is an extension of what already exists, the move will be easier than if it is one in which a major change in direction is expected. Before moving forward, you may want to first assess whether the competencies needed to implement the plan are present and available.

Most organizations can no longer support a large cadre of middle managers. Profitability comes when fewer people are required to do the work and everyone pulls a heavier load. People must not only have the required technical expertise, they must also be able to relate well to others. If people have neither the technical skills nor the interpersonal skills, the resources are not available to implement the idea. The leader must understand how the new idea will change the company and the many ways in which people will need to work together.

Assessing an organization's readiness for change can be daunting. After more than 20 years of experience working in organizations, we still find the assessment phase difficult. People who appear to embrace the change will nevertheless resist implementing it because they lack the necessary professional or personal capabilities. On the other hand, people who appear incapable of change will rise to the occasion. The leader's ability to assess the competence to successfully implement the change is a critical ingredient of long-term success. Questions of competence include not only the abilities of followers, but also the leader's ability to lead and operate in changed circumstances. The following questions are designed to assess competence and the organization's readiness to undertake an envisioned change in direction.

Leadership Competencies

- What kind of leadership will be required in the future? How is such leadership similar/different from the way I am most comfortable operating? What does this mean for me?
- What messages must I deliver? What is my communications plan?
- What do I need to learn? Who will help me learn it?

Organizational Competencies

- How must people work together? Will it be different from their accustomed ways? How can I ensure that people will collaborate to achieve the change?
- What new approaches or technical skills may be required? What is the best way to ensure that people learn new skills and use them?
- What have we learned from our past successes and mistakes? What do past successes tell us about how we might want to move forward?
- Have we the right people on staff to affect the change?

Although you may be eager to begin moving forward with your new project, it may be helpful to ensure that your people are ready to implement. They may not need to possess all the required competencies before the project starts, but how long will it take to obtain them? See Chapters 4 and 5 for more information on building competencies.

Implementing the Direction

Leaders become excited during the conceptual and the learning phases of a transition. New possibilities are invigorating. But the day of implementation often brings sheer panic. Do we really believe that this project will bring the expected results? What if something goes wrong? Suppose things don't work out, what will happen to my career? My investment? What negative impact might this have on employees? What will happen to my business?

A while ago a leader we knew had thoroughly prepared for a major organizational change, involved employees with the planning, and felt ready to move forward—or so he thought. The day he announced that he would begin to move in the new direction he became uncharacteristically hostile toward all around him. Beneath the surface was sheer panic. He knew the risks to the organization and the people in it. Although many people had significantly contributed to the plan, he felt accountable if the objectives were not attained. Though many around him shared his passion and had contributed their best thinking to the plan, this leader knew he was ultimately alone.

During implementation people must not only talk about the right things; they must also do the right things. Doing requires higher levels of communication and coordination than talking. People must be held accountable for promised accomplishments. During implementation, we discover whatever we didn't or couldn't know earlier. Our true leadership capabilities emerge during the heat of the implementation phase. Idealism strikes against reality, and we are forced to make choices and compromises that we might wish to ignore.

When evaluating whether you and the organization are prepared to move forward to the implementation phase ask:

- Even though we will be better off for implementing the new idea, what will people have to give up?
- How might existing policies, procedures, practices, and processes get in the way of implementation? What will I need to do about this?
- What new processes will have to be put in place to make the idea work? Examples include human resources, finance, and information systems.
- What if the project takes twice as long, costs twice as much, becomes twice as large as we originally thought? What will be the impact?

- How might this project become derailed? How will I deal with barriers? Who or what will resist this effort?
- Am I discounting a potential problem by thinking that others do not have the capability to hurt the project? What will I do if incompetence stops or harms the project?

Map Assessment

Raising and answering the above questions are critical to the success of your leadership of the project or transformation you wish to undertake. If you believe that a more formal assessment would be of value to you, Appendix A contains a survey that does not measure organizational climate, employee satisfaction, or the strengths/weaknesses of an individual. It does measure the leadership function. It asks respondents to assess organizational requirements, environmental influences, and project execution. Scoring responses on the grid will help determine organizational needs and required leadership improvement.

Costs of Ignoring the Map

The leadership team of a nationally known insurance company emerged from their annual planning session with an exciting new direction. They decided that the organization needed to broaden its product line and to deliver services in new ways. Under the new scheme, customers would no longer receive all their insurance advice from one person. Instead they would have several "advisors," each with different expertise. To accomplish the change, a new sales compensation program would have to be designed to encourage joint sales ownership for customers. The Human Resources Department was charged with the responsibility of devising the new sales compensation plan. Unfortunately, the sales organization heard about the potential changes and squelched not only the change in the compensation plan, but also the goal to sell the expanded insurance program. Clearly leaders had moved from reframing the future to building community without first developing commitment or teaching and learning. Clearly the insurance industry was going through a very significant metamorphosis, but the sales organization had handcuffed the leadership team and significantly affected the long-term viability of this company.

The mistakes made by the leadership team of the insurance company are all too common. Consensus within the leadership team regarding a future direction does not ensure that the concept is sound or can be implemented. It will take significant thinking, planning, selling, developing, allocating, attempting, and re-attempting to make the new idea work for the long term. Had the group been more aware of the steps outlined in the Leader's Map, they might have avoided a serious setback.

Early in his career, one of the authors was involved in the major transformation of a division within a Fortune 500 organization. He sought to transform the organization from one in which employees operated independently to one in which they had mutual accountability in a strong team environment. The change was well thought through, the employees stated their strong commitment to the process, and much attention was given to building the infrastructure. Unfortunately, the project did not proceed as planned. Although the employees stated that they wanted to operate in a team environment, they were unwilling to give up their autonomy. What the architects of the transformation failed to appreciate was the dilemma of people wanting both individual freedom and recognition and wanting to work together in a coordinated fashion. Had the author possessed the Leader's Map at the time, he might have predicted some of the difficulties that emerged later, when the organization was well into implementing the change.

The Leader's Map may help you anticipate some of the obstacles that could keep the organization from moving forward and what you will need to do.

Whose Job Is It to Lead?

Leadership does not have to be a solo act. A group of people, working closely together, can provide the deliverables of direction, ensuring competence, and ensuring that change is implemented. To do so requires participants to share similar values, to develop a commitment to each other and the organization, and to allow those who possess complementary skills to lead when appropriate.

People learn by doing. The tools in this book encourage collaboration, dialogue, joint decision making, and action. Working together to address the most central issues of a company creates teamwork, mutual accountability, and the ability to achieve greatness.

Summary

In this chapter, we have defined what leaders do and provided opportunities to develop insight when implementing major organizational changes. The five leadership challenges are reviewed in Table 1-1.

Table 1-1: Explanation of the Five Leadership Challenges

Challenge	Purpose
Reframe the Future	Establish a strategy that repositions the company to take advantage of its strengths, redefine relationships with key partners, revolutionize how the product is produced or delivered to customers, and create new products and services
Develop Commitment	Develop a critical mass of supporters who understand the strategy and will do what is necessary to succeed
Teach and Learn	Develop the leadership skills needed to move the organization forward. Build competence in people throughout the organization. Establish processes that encourage learning to undertake new challenges now and into the future.
Build Community	Create the infrastructure that enables people to work together effectively and accomplish the expected results
Balance Paradox	Build in the mechanisms to manage the conflicts that naturally occur when reality collides with expectations

At certain times in the organization's life, some challenges are more important than others. Know where the organization is and what is needed. Then focus on the appropriate challenges.

Organizational leadership is a function, one that may be attended to by a single person, a small group, or many people throughout the organization who care about what can be achieved. Who does what to meet leadership responsibilities depends on what the organization needs and who possesses the skills to meet those needs.

Managers ensure order and consistency. They delegate tasks, solve problems, and ensure that expectations are fulfilled. Leaders ensure the long-term health of their organizations by meeting the five leadership challenges.

Many leaders are more comfortable being individual contributors or managers than they are fulfilling their leadership responsibilities. Most people have spent most of their time learning the specific technologies of their profession.

Organizations are more likely to have programs in place to encourage managership than leadership. What is expected from leaders is unclear.

The Leader's Map provides a path for thinking about and implementing change. Problems will occur if the leader moves directly from reframe the future to build community without first attending to issues of commitment and competency.

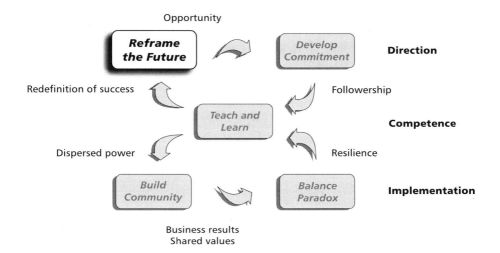

Opportunity

Reframe the Future

Develop Commitment — **Direction**

Redefinition of success

Teach and Learn

Followership — **Competence**

Dispersed power

Resilience

Build Community — **Balance Paradox** — **Implementation**

Business results
Shared values

CHAPTER 2

Reframe the Future

> In business, as in art, what distinguishes leaders from laggards, and greatness from mediocrity, is the ability to uniquely imagine what could be.
>
> —*Gary Hamel and C.K. Prahlahad*

> The real voyage of discovery lies not in seeking new lands, but in having new eyes.
>
> —*Marcel Proust*

Shopping Centers USA provides consulting advice, retail space, management and administrative staff, maintenance and security, and marketing for large shopping centers throughout the United

States. In return for these services mall owners and retailers pay significant administrative and management fees. Shopping Centers USA's long history enables the group to establish relationships with mall owners and large national retailers. In addition to their excellent understanding of the marketplace, their conservative compensation and the efficient manner in which they operate the properties ensure a profitable return.

Triple Five Corporation, architects of the largest mall in the world in Edmonton, Canada, targeted Minneapolis, Minnesota, where Shopping Centers USA managed four malls, including Eastdale, one of its most profitable properties. Triple Five envisioned the largest shopping center in the world, one that would offer unparalleled amenities. Their megamall would be more than a place to shop—it would be a total entertainment experience.

Shopping Centers USA's leadership remained unconcerned about the new mall. They dubbed the project a "megamistake." They "knew" the large debt service, the initial low rates offered to the anchor stores, the layout of the facility, the marketing expenses, and the large number of talented employees required to operate the facility would lead to the new mall's eventual demise. Unfortunately history proved otherwise. Six years after its construction, the Mall of America remains economically strong. More than 600,000 shoppers visit the mall in a typical week, and 37 percent of the shoppers come from outside a 150-mile radius to participate in the experience. The mall, which is more than 92 percent occupied, has been a colossal success! Additional entertainment and retail facilities are planned.

Shopping Centers USA's Eastdale, for the first time in its history, has experienced vacancies and falling retail revenue. The value of the property has been downgraded despite a recent renovation.

How is it possible that the leaders of a successful enterprise could so underestimate the threat of a competitor? That's easy to answer! They failed to understand that the Triple Five Corporation was changing the rules, as shown in Table 2-1.

Shopping Centers USA did not foresee the emergence of a different reality. To have done so would have required abandoning many valuable lessons learned through the school of hard knocks.

Table 2-1: Comparison of Shopping Centers USA and Triple Five Corporation Assumptions

Shopping Center USA's Operating Principles	*Triple Five's Operating Principles*
Build it and they will come	Make it interesting enough, and they will come
A mall is a place to shop	A mall is a place to play, shop, dine, and learn
A mall draws shoppers from a relatively defined regional area	A mall draws shoppers from anywhere on the globe
Employees are expendable and easy to replace	Employees are integral to the organization's success and should be trained and compensated accordingly
Amusement facilities are unprofitable	Amusement facilities are core attractions
The mall owes the local community nothing	The mall operates as an integral part of the local community

Determined not to replicate past mistakes, the company had established unwritten rules to guide its behaviors. For example, early attempts to add recreational facilities had failed. The leaders could not conceive that several nightclubs, a walk-through aquarium, an amusement park, a 12-screen movie theater, and a wedding chapel would be economically viable. They believed that drive-time limited the numbers of people who would frequent the mall, which would in turn limit the scope and size of the mall. They saw employees as an expense rather than as a source of differentiation. The leadership of Shopping Centers USA looked upon the Triple Five Corporation's proposal as foolhardy.

Imagine that you are an executive of the Triple Five Corporation. You are handed a budget of 650 million dollars and instructed to construct a building of 4.2 million square feet, of which 2.5 million square feet is retail space. You are to hire more than 11,000 employees. You might wonder what the boss had been smoking. Yet this outlandish thinking changed the marketplace.

Like Triple Five, much of the value you bring to your leadership role is your judgment. What will you do when it is your turn to create the future? How will you know when it is time to change the rules? How will you establish a range of possibilities? How will you evaluate the threat of the next competitor to address the wants and needs of your customers? How will you know if you are being rational or overly ambitious? How will you know if your perspective is what is needed or if it will lead to your organization's eventual demise?

Jim, whom we met in the introduction, is like many leaders. He assessed the health of his organization simply by reviewing the balance sheet and the profit and loss and cash flow statements. He did not realize that standard accounting practices provide grand testimony to a company's historical achievements—and almost no insight into future possibilities. When a leader focuses on financial measures, this is analogous to driving while looking only in the rearview mirror. Jim understood the inadequacy of his assessment, but he had little other reliable data. Unfortunately, the board's wholehearted support of his decision to reduce the payroll alleviated the short-term pain, but it also threatened the long-term success of the company.

Reframe the Future

Leaders constantly strive to improve the value of their organization's products and services to customers. They reframe the future by changing the fundamental rules of the industry, creating new industries, altering critical relationships.

Changing the Fundamental Rules of the Industry

Leaders in a given industry have learned that an established set of standardized business practices will likely lead to a successful result. A new entrant into the industry may conceive of quite a different way to exceed customer expectations. For example, Triple Five's Mall of America has thrown the market for the existing malls out of balance. Existing malls must respond to the threat.

Another example of changing the rules is Wal-Mart, which demanded a much closer partnership with its suppliers, resulting in cost savings for both Wal-Mart and its customers. Thus, a new structure has fundamentally changed traditional customer/supplier relationships. Sun Country Airlines, too, has challenged the conventional wisdom of the large hub-and-spoke carriers. It found efficiencies in providing air service directly to destinations. A Sun Country plane travels back and forth to the same cities several times a day, providing the airlines and its passengers with significant savings. The company's lower fares challenge the larger carriers to lower prices and their profits.

Creating New Industries

Ten years ago, few of us owned personal computers, wore pagers, walked anywhere we wanted with a telephone, listened to compact discs, or cropped and printed photographs on our computers. These products are the work of visionary leaders who possessed the foresight and the courage to allocate the required resources and to nurture the process of development. Their genius was the ability to visualize the connections between emerging technologies and improved products and services for their customers. The leaders generated these products by utilizing their organization's capabilities in new ways by funding a number of small investments. When their small investments were linked together, they created opportunities not previously imaginable.

Changing/Establishing Relationships and Capabilities

Flattening the organizational structure, encouraging people to work in cross-functional teams, encouraging employees to explore new opportunities, and changing the compensation structure to encourage risk taking are the means by which leaders refocus organizational talent. In the last several years, it has become apparent that getting employees to work together to pool their intelligence and talents is a significant weapon for creating competitive advantage.

When an organization does not have the internal capability to achieve a strategic objective, it can partner with one that does.

When the partnership proves to be successful, both companies can achieve results that would not have been possible if they operated separately. Companies today cooperate to create strategic advantage by reducing supply costs, gaining access to new markets, shortening the time from concept to market, offering a significantly better product, developing new operational processes, and gaining efficiencies of scale.

Common Factors That Keep Leaders from Redefining the Map

Despite their intellectual understanding of the need for continuous innovation, what keeps leaders from innovating?

Lack of Tools to See the Field

Leaders are well aware of the actions of their most formidable competitors. Most pay particular attention to an array of competitors with whom they feel an intense rivalry. Unfortunately, narrow and intense scrutiny of known competitors often causes leaders to underestimate the threat of new competitors or to undervalue the power of new technologies. Seldom do leaders have the tools or do they take the time to lay out the playing field visually on a map, which would allow them to challenge existing thought and defuse emotions.

Inability to Identify Where the Company Is on the Map

As the examples of Shopping Centers USA and Jim demonstrate, knowing when to encourage significant change is certainly a tricky matter. It is impossible to know when a process or technology that has worked well in the past is no longer effective. Leaders typically lack the tools to identify where their organization is within its life cycle. Lacking such knowledge, the leader is unsure if continuous evolutionary improvements are appropriate or if completely new, discontinuous changes are required. Discontinuous change cannot be predicted from trends. It is a new pattern, one that enables what may once have been an impossibility to become reality.

Inability to Conceive the Map in New Ways

Their inability to visualize the world in new ways forces leaders to extrapolate a future from what currently exists. In general, leaders assume that present circumstances will prevail in the future. Redefining the map enhances the ability to see the industry in new perspectives. Expanding the list of possibilities enhances leaders' decision making.

Lack of Internal Competence

Some leaders wait to make required changes or to explore new options because they believe they lack the organizational talent and the financial resources to do so. They believe that exploring new technologies, markets, products, will require people to work differently, which creates demands on leaders, who already have plates piled high with difficult challenges.

Inability to Move Forward When the Answers Are Unknowable

Because no investment, decision, or strategy is guaranteed to be successful, leaders often deal with the unknowable. Regardless of the comprehensiveness of an analysis or the solidity of a consensus, any decision to move toward change risks failure. Leaders often opt to maintain the status quo rather than dare to make a mistake.

Consequences of Failure to Reframe the Future

Leaders who fail to reframe the future put their companies at risk. Then, when competitors change industry rules, leaders feel pressured to make quick decisions rather than to look for more fundamentally effective ways of operating. They may initiate new strategies to overcome their competition, rather than thinking through a number of options and making decisions that solidify their long-term future; they simply react—and later change their minds. Soon their employees begin to think their leaders are asking everyone to participate in a flavor-of-the month fad. Vital energy dissipates. The organization fails to gain the momentum it needs to compete.

Leaders sometimes attempt to mitigate risks by managing the business more closely. They shut down unprofitable divisions; they manage their direct reports more closely; they slash budgets and hamstring innovation. These activities may be necessary and valuable in the short-term, but they are not all related to reframing the future. Thus, they are unlikely to ensure the long-term health of the organization.

In this chapter we provide analytical and creative methods to create the map of your industry, to identify where your organization is in its growth cycle, and to identify several approaches to creating a new reality for your company.

Exercise: Design the Perfect Frog

Staff meetings and leadership development programs are wonderful venues for completing this exercise. If a group is unavailable, you may wish to take 10 minutes to complete the exercise on your own before you read the remainder of this chapter.

Imagine that you and your colleagues are well-known biologists. You have been commissioned by Congress to design the perfect frog. The result of your work will be used to improve the health and welfare of frogs across the United States. In the next 10 to 15 minutes, determine where to start and how to change the frog. At this time, do not be concerned how you might achieve your ideas. When you are finished, describe your proposed changes and the rationale for each change.

Laying Out the Playing Field

Newly designed frogs typically are more colorful, evoke more sonorous ribbits, exhibit greater leaping power, or have increased sexual prowess. These are worthy attributes, but of what value are they to the frog? The perfect design for the frog requires a complete under-

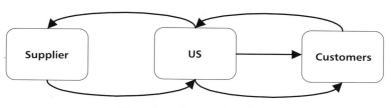

Figure 2-1: Customer-Supplier Relationship

standing of the ecosystem in which the frog exists. If the frog cannot adapt to changes in its environment, its long-term survival is at risk. Inexplicable changes in the environment are currently threatening a number of frog species around the world. So much for our human ability to design what nature has taken years to achieve.

Similarly, the leader's activities that reduce cost, enhance product and service capability, position the organization in new ways, and so on are meritorious only to the degree that they enhance the organization's ability to prosper within its ecosystem. The leader's first challenge is to define the ecosystem and to ensure that critical stakeholders understand it.

All businesses have customers and suppliers, as shown in Figure 2-1. In a typical transaction, customers define expectations, find value in what is being offered, and pay money in return. Most organizations cannot sustain themselves without offering value to their customers. On the other hand, most organizations rely on suppliers to help them produce their products and services. Enhanced supplier relationships add significantly to a company's ability to achieve its objectives.

Most customers have alternate products and services that could be suitable substitutes. For example, when changing the oil in your car, both natural oils and synthetics are available. If the price of oranges is too high, then apples may do. The attractiveness of the organization's offerings could be challenged by competitors who are more recent entrants to the market. New competitors may

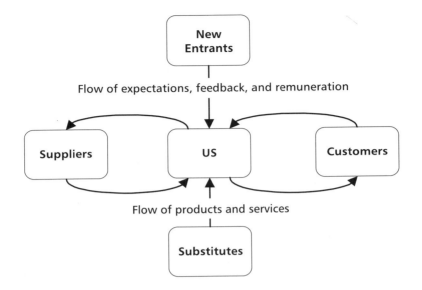

Figure 2-2: Suppliers, Customers, New Entrants, and Substitutions (Reproduced by permission from Porter, 1980)

be able to offer improved and/or less costly products and challenge the relationship with existing customers. The existence of new entrants and substitutes is illustrated in Figure 2-2.

Exercise: Build the Relationship Map

This exercise provides a basis to analyze your current competitive position and establish future possibilities. Below are the first steps to use in defining your organization's ecosystem. Many leaders find the completion of this exercise both more difficult and more rewarding than they expected. Whenever possible, choose to ask customers and suppliers directly for their perspectives.

Step 1   **Defining Your Customers**
- Who are your customers?
- What do they receive from you?
- What do you get in return?
- Why do they buy from you?

Step 2 **Assessing Your Customers—Current Situation**
- Who are your most profitable customers? Why?
- Who are your least profitable customers? Why?
- What do you look like from your customers' perspectives?
- Why do they use *your* product or service?
- How do the customers use your product/service?
- What do your customers wish for from your product/service?
- What might make your product/service obsolete?
- What changes are or will be occurring in your customer's business? How might they affect your business?
- If you could make three changes to the product/service you provide, what would your customers like them to be?

Step 3 **Assessing Your Customers—Future Situation**
- Who else would you like to serve? What keeps you from doing so?
- If you could make minor changes in your products/services, who else could you serve?

Step 4 **Defining Your Suppliers**
- Who are your major suppliers?
- What do you receive from them?
- What do they get in return?
- Why do you do business with these particular suppliers?

Step 5 **Assessing Your Suppliers**
- How would your suppliers define the relationship they have with you?
- How well do you communicate expectations of each other?
- What do you do internally that might better be performed by an outside vendor?
- What could you do to improve the performance of and relationship with critical suppliers?

Step 6 **Understanding Substitutions**
- If your product/service were unavailable, what would your customers do?

- What changes in technology, market forces, regulations, and so on might make your product obsolete?

Step 7   **Broadening Awareness of New Entrants**
- Who else might serve our customers?
- What capabilities do the new entrants or existing competition have that our customers might prefer or that might reduce margins?
- How would new entrants into the marketplace appear to your customers?

Step 8   **Draw "As Is" Map**
- Integrate the answers and create a current organizational map similar to the figure below. Notice two-way relationships with customers and suppliers. The arrow from your organization to your customer or supplier describes what you give, and the arrow in the other direction describes what you get.
- Place potential new entrants on your map. Also place the substitutions. These are potential threats and external constraints to your business growth.
- (Please note the Ralph's Hamburger Joint example in Figure 2-3.)

Step 9   **Analyze the Map**
- What new customers might be interested in your existing products and services?
- What improvements would customers like in price, quality, service, and innovation?
- How could you utilize your suppliers more effectively?
- With which suppliers do you have good relationships and not so good relationships? Should you change suppliers?
- Will new competitors or substitutes have a significant impact on your customers—why or why not?

Step 10   **Sorting Through the Information**
It may be helpful to place the data from the above analysis into a table/matrix. Examples of topics are:
- Risk versus opportunity

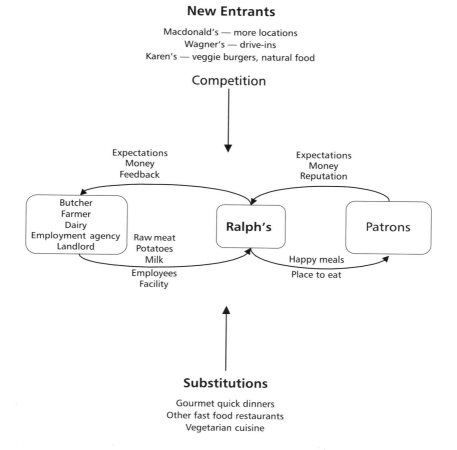

New Entrants

Macdonald's — more locations
Wagner's — drive-ins
Karen's — veggie burgers, natural food

Competition

Expectations
Money
Feedback

Expectations
Money
Reputation

Butcher
Farmer
Dairy
Employment agency
Landlord

Ralph's

Patrons

Raw meat
Potatoes
Milk

Happy meals
Place to eat

Employees
Facility

Substitutions

Gourmet quick dinners
Other fast food restaurants
Vegetarian cuisine

Figure 2-3: An Example of an External Relationship Map of Ralph's Hamburger Joint

- Degree of change required versus reward expected
- Capabilities we have versus capabilities we need

The example in Table 2-2 demonstrates what the matrix might look like.

Step 11   **Possible Next Steps**

- What are the major things we should do to improve our business?

Table 2-2: Comparison of Required Capabilities vs. Current Capabilities

		Current Capabilities	
		Low	*High*
Required Capabilities	*High*		
	Low		

- What organizations might we partner with that would enable us to completely change the industry?
- How might we organize to better use the talents that currently exist inside the company?

Step 12   **Analyze**

Figure 2-3 represents the completed relationship map for Ralph's Hamburger Joint. The business has existed for a number of years and is recognized for its ability to offer "Hamburgers for all tastes and occasions."

As the managers of Ralph's Hamburger Joint reflected on the map, they reached several startling conclusions. Several years ago the organization had decided to market its product to people with more sophisticated palates. Many of its targeted customers were moving toward vegetarian diets. Others were purchasing more fast food in grocery stores. Drive-ins offered variety for customers in the summertime. Competing with high-quality offerings would be insufficient. Further study of the map indicated opportunities to sell to corporate clients who were tired of pizza. Ralph's decided on an experiment. They would offer delivered meals to business people, and catering for company events. Ralph's had a positive image in the community, and the map showed that expanding service options was a way to expand its customer base.

Where Are You on the Map?

People and organizations are born, develop, mature, and die. Leaders extend the life and profitability of their companies by knowing when to focus on organizational renewal and reinvention.

Until the sextant was developed, ancient sailors could not travel great distances because they had no way of knowing their location. This concept seems strange to us, but imagine you are driving from Malaga, New Jersey, to Laguna Hills, California. If you don't know where Malaga is, getting to California will be difficult. Leaders sometimes base important decisions on incomplete information about where their organization is in its life cycle. Such leaders risk making decisions that will lead to great difficulties in keeping the organization alive.

The S curve, which describes the natural progression of most companies through their growth cycles, provides insight into the leader's roles associated with each phase, which are described below. The phases of the S curve and the leadesr' roles are illustrated in Figure 2-4.

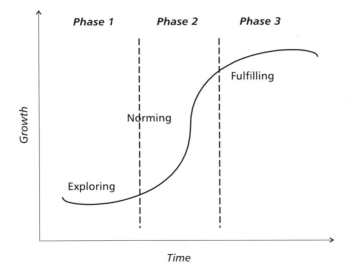

Figure 2-4: The S Curve of Organizational Growth (Adapted from Land, Jarman, 1992)

Phase 1: Exploring

During Phase 1, the leader discovers what is possible and establishes a blueprint for the future through experimentation and invention. Leaders and employees create as they go, adapting to unpredictable circumstances and insufficient people and financial resources. Despite the hardships, there is much excitement about future possibilities. The entrepreneurial leader bends the rules and adapts to an emerging and exciting reality. Companies that are successful during Phase 1 have a strong foundation for future growth.

Phase 2: Norming

The blueprint established in Phase 1 now requires discipline for its implementation. The chaos that was required for first phase development must now give way to order. The entrepreneur who continues to develop new products does not give the organization time to formalize and standardize its processes. During this phase the traditional management functions of planning, organizing, controlling, and measuring are required to stabilize the company. As people develop standard routines and responsibilities and the level of predictability increases, their stress levels decrease. At this stage, the company is considered successful when customers' expectations can uniformly be fulfilled and profit achieved.

Also during this phase, leaders encourage employees to undertake small, low-risk innovations that provide opportunities in areas the organization already knows. A series of insignificant innovations may lead to increased competence or to entrance in new markets that may be critical for the organization's long-term success.

Because the organization has more time and resources available, it may experiment with new ways for people to work together. Examples include teams, flattening the organization's hierarchy, improving processes, and training programs.

Phase 3: Fulfilling

Over time, the very forces that brought success in Phase 2 will lead to a plateau. Organizations may experience:

- Greater competition from other organizations who deliver similar products and services at lower cost or higher quality
- Large increases in people and financial resources needed to achieve even modest gains in productivity
- Greater internal competition for resources
- Reduction in market share
- A substitute product or new technology that significantly reduces customers' need for the product

Despite changing circumstances, employees, who value security, may initially resist actions to counter the threats. They maintain existing standardizations for their own sake rather than trying new practices. What may once have been innovative is no longer. More resources are required to achieve marginal productivity improvements. Competitors or new entrants threaten the core business. New organizational initiatives are required to overcome the inertia. Many existing employees resist the new, believing that more attention to fundamental management principles will enable the organization to return to previous levels of success. The leader must juggle the continuation of the existing core business with the development of the new business, and ensure the flow of resources between them. The organization may need to find partners who possess new necessary competencies or access to new markets. The complexity of Phase 3 presents a great leadership challenge. It is in Phase 3 that the leader realizes the fundamental rules of the playing field are about to be rewritten.

As the leader initiates change, resources are reallocated from the existing business to the new. Employees find themselves in a precarious environment. Those working on the delivery of existing products will be concerned with job security and will resent any changes made to the business. Other employees may be called upon to and develop the new. Resistance from employees may cause leaders to question their own rationale.

Figure 2-5 uses two S curves to illustrate discontinuous change as the organization develops the next growth cycle. The flash point occurs within the shaded area, when the organization must balance what appear to be conflicting courses of action. Table

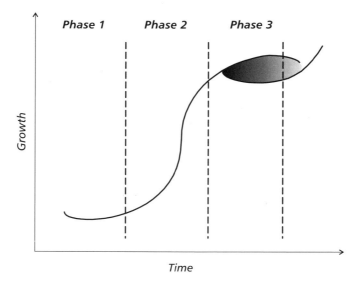

Figure 2-5: Existing and New S Curves

2-3 describes the leadership challenges and transition issues that occur during the three phases of the S curve.

Exercise: Build Your Organization's S Curve

This exercise focuses on your organization's growth curve, although you could also create one that describes your career. Remember that multiple S curves on one graph are possible. The exercise will be more successfully completed if others participate.

Step 1   Develop a table with three headings entitled "Year," "Accomplishments," and "Issues."
      • In the left-hand column write each year from the inception of the organization to the present.
      • For each year, complete the table and write the major accomplishments and issues to address.

Step 2   Create the S curve by drawing a graph with a line for the x-axis (Growth) and one for the y-axis (Time). Note the

Table 2-3: Leader Challenges and Transition Issues by Phase

Phase	Challenges	Transition Issues
Phase 1: Forming	• Explore opportunities with a new set of eyes • Manage the range of emotions from exuberance to fear • Create a balance between the dream and the resources required to achieve it • Keep people interested enough to make commitments	• Stay with the business concept long enough to bring to fruition • Achieve balance between what is achievable and what is an unachievable dream • Know when to move from concept to implementation
Phase 2: Norming	• Establish an achievable agenda • Install management practices • Communicate regularly • Ensure commitments are achieved • Allocate resources effectively • Improve productivity • Standardize product/service and the processes used to create them	• Maintain the balance between continued innovation and efficiency • Maintain an open culture • Respond to changes in customer expectations • Use financial measurements as the only/prime method of assessing organizational health
Phase 3: Fulfilling	• Be personally open to the need for major change • Help others overcome resistance to change • Provide organizational structure and resources to explore and realize new products and services • Manage a stressful political organizational climate • Retrain and retool the assets of the corporation • Establish a new vision and sell it	• Know what and when to unlearn • Create space where employees feel empowered to innovate • Find a critical mass of leaders who will support the change effort • Find the courage to overcome personal doubts and setbacks • Know when and how to ask for support • Create strategic partnerships • Successfully manage the core business and invent the new business

years on the y-axis. For each year, plot where you believe the company was or is on the growth axis. Remember that the straight lines are an approximation over time. Yearly differences indicate a trend over time. Draw the line for your S curve or curves.

Step 3   Determine your current position on the S curve and mark it.

- What leadership challenges are suggested by your position on the S curve?
- What product and service challenges are suggested by the curve?
- Are you at a point that requires a change from one phase to another?

Step 4   Develop a story to describe the journey that the company is on, using the terminology of the S curve.

- Tell others the story, and see if they agree with your perspective.
- What will you do to help the organization continue to move forward?

Example: Combining the External Relationship Map and the S Curve

At an age when most of us would consider retiring, David Prosser had a compelling dream: to revolutionize the worker's compensation system in the United States. For several years he owned a home health-care company and designed home treatments for back-pain patients. Although he offered a valuable service, few patients sought out David's assistance. Surprised by the lack of a more favorable customer response, he sought the counsel of a physician friend, who helped David realize that backaches could often be attributed to drugs, job dissatisfaction, destructive relationships, or unhappy marriages. The longer the patient was away from work, the more likely he or she would become entrapped in a negative situation. Prosser's reframing of the industry revealed that conflicting relationships between employer, insurance companies, hospitals, and physicians unwittingly encouraged many employees to extend their leaves. The result was higher employer premiums. None of the major stakeholders was satisfied. Clearly, the industry was in Phase 3.

Prosser sold his assets and started a new company, RTW, which stands for return to work. RTW's mission was to reduce the adversarial nature of the workers compensation system, to save money, to get people back to work more quickly, and, most important, to save patients from a downward spiral of dependence. David's new company broke well-established industry rules. He provided advocates to represent client companies, he created liaisons with physicians to develop bridges between client companies and patients. And he fostered relationships with insurance companies to ensure that claims were properly managed. All would be expected to work together as a team to ensure that proper arrangements were made to get workers back to work as soon as possible, even if it meant they would be assigned lighter responsibilities. RTW gained an excellent reputation and took significant business away from more traditional insurance companies.

Years later, other companies have successfully emulated the RTW model. What was once a revolutionary idea has now become a Phase 2 norm. The change in rules initiated by RTW appears in Table 2-4.

Table 2-4: Comparison of Existing Industry Practice and RTW's Approach

Existing Industry Approach	*RTW's Approach*
Stakeholders maximize their own interests.	Bring the parties together for the mutual benefit of the employee.
The physician will determine when the employee is ready to return to work.	Get the worker back to work as soon as possible by negotiating and collaborating with the employer, physician, and insurance company to ensure a win for all parties.
Stakeholders operate independently.	An existing team of functional specialists works together to resolve the workers' issues.

RTW is particularly interesting because Prosser's major reframing was to get stakeholders to work as a team on behalf of the worker. RTW spent significant time training its employees to work in self-empowered teams and allowed them the freedom to do so once they demonstrated competence. Similarly, Triple Five Corporation defined the importance of employees who are committed to excellent service, and the company established training programs to ensure that mall visitors would have an excellent experience.

Imagine that it is 1985 and you are determining whether to invest in the company on the left- or right-hand side below. Which company in each pair would you have chosen?

Volkswagon/Honda
Upjohn/Glaxo
CBS/CNN
RCA/Sony
Westinghouse/Hitachi
Sears/Wal-Mart
(Hamel, Prahalad, 1994)

The organizations in the left-hand column were extremely successful, operated with integrity, hired bright and capable people, and possessed sufficient resources. Their decline in the marketplace was most likely due to the manner in which employees were inspired, focused, and led. It was due to their inability to evolve as their market ecosystems changed. In retrospect it is easy to see what should have been done. Leaders should have challenged existing assumptions and created new thinking and new capabilities in time to ensure the long-term health of the company. They should have reframed the organization.

Developing Alternative Futures

Experience and education shape what leaders believe is possible. Unfortunately, the past is not always a useful predictor of the future. Knowing what to unlearn and how to look at the world through different glasses are major challenges. The process of building scenarios offers leaders and employees an opportunity to understand the forces that shape organizational success, to create options based on unfolding events, and to perceive the organization in new ways. Scenarios are a set of reasonably plausible, but structurally different futures (Van der Heijden, p. 29). Scenarios do not predict the future. They create a range of possibilities. Leaders who participate in building scenarios together are better able to adapt and proactively operate within the organization's ecosystem.

When they have completed a scenario-building process, they will have:

- Determined the most critical issues for the organization
- Developed an understanding of the forces that are likely to affect the organization's success
- Established a wide range of options
- Deepened their understanding of what could be accomplished and why

Selecting Participants

Because scenario building requires a significant time commitment, it is best to involve those who have an interest in learning and a passion for their organization's success. Select a diverse group of participants to ensure that an honest and well-rounded result will be achieved. It is useful to select three teams with four to five members each.

An outside facilitator or someone skilled in group facilitation, problem solving, and planning is required to lead the scenario-building process. The leader works closely with the facilitator to ensure that objectives are understood and support is available.

Setting the Stage

Participants are told that scenario building is a learning exercise that could have a profound impact on the organization. Norms for working together are established:

- We are here to deal in current reality and establish possibilities for the future.

- Opposing viewpoints belong here and will be honored in our dialogue.
- We will include knowledge that resides outside the company.
- We will take the long-term view.
- We are here to deepen our knowledge.
- Sacred cows are fair game.

Developing the Question

Knowing what to discuss is difficult. Ask each team the following questions:

- If you encountered a sage, what two questions would you want answered?
- What would a desirable scenario look like?
- What would an undesirable scenario look like?
- If you could go back to the founding of the organization, what would you have liked to have known?
- What are the most important decisions we must now make?
- What internal constraints prevent us from becoming successful?
- What are we doing now that will help us become more successful?
- What do we want our stakeholders to say about our company?

(Adapted from Senge, Kleiner, Roberts, Ross, Smith, 1994)

Based on the responses to these eight challenging questions, each team develops a question they deem to be critical to the company's future. The teams then share their thinking and formulate a single question, the answer to which could profoundly affect the future of the organization. Such questions could be as follows:

- What could make our product obsolete?
- How can we use our particular strengths to greater advantage?
- How can we change customer perceptions of our company?
- What would it take to improve the company culture?
- What does leadership mean to us and for the organization?

- What do we risk in becoming a different kind of company?
- What will our industry look like in three years?
- Who should our company partner with and why?
- Which of our competitors seems to be going in the wrong direction?
- How is our industry similar to another industry? What happened in that industry that could happen to us? What should we do?

Establishing Driving Forces

A number of factors influence the question we choose to answer. For example, the obsolescence of product or service might come as a result of declining demand, a need for more economical production methods, a substitute product or service, and so on. The team investigating this issue must start with the idea that at some point the market demand for the product or service will cease. It also must imagine the circumstances that could drastically lower demand. Each team is asked to define what might influence such a result. Typical areas of change include:

> Society
> Technology
> Economics
> Politics
> Environment
>> (Schwartz, 1996)

For each change, team members might ask:

- Where will we find good information about this area?
- What are the major trends in each change?
- What impact will changes have on our industry? On our organization? On us?
- How could we use these changes to our advantage?
- How certain are we that these changes will happen?
- Which changes are important to us? Which are not?
- What additional information will be important for us to have?

Creating Stories

Stories help listeners perceive situations from both emotional and logical perspectives. They allow listeners to momentarily suspend assumptions and explore possibilities. Effective stories contain three essential ingredients: setting the context, laying out the dramatic conflict, and resolving the conflict.

Setting the Context

Listeners need to know the current organization and how it evolved. The storyteller describes the current situation (e.g., the map, the S curve), the driving forces, the rationale for significant decisions, specific historical events and their impact on the business, and so on. The storyteller concludes with the issues that are of special concern. The storyteller provides the opportunity for listeners to ask questions and deepen their knowledge of the organization through discussion with others. Examples of organizations in similar situations could deepen listeners' learning and understanding.

Laying Out the Dramatic Conflict

The storyteller shares alternate possibilities for the organization and focuses on the gap between the current state and the desired state. This creates the tension that fuels the active involvement of the listener. The storyteller concludes this portion with a series of questions to address. The storyteller knows that participants must experience sufficient emotional discomfort to become engaged in the drama and to understand that a new course of action is required.

Finding Resolution

The storyteller charges the listeners to find solutions to the dramatic conflict that has been presented. The groups use both analytical and nonanalytical approaches. They are encouraged to find examples outside their immediate organization. The storyteller charges the groups to be creative in their approaches and in their resolutions. Each group subsequently develops a plan, describing in detail the resolution to the dramatic conflict. They then become the storytellers.

Presenting Stories

Each team is instructed to develop a story about an assigned theme using the format described above, that is, establishing the context, laying out the dramatic conflict, and finding resolution. Participants are seated in two concentric circles. It is beneficial not to use tables. The inner circle is composed of the storyteller group. The outer circle consists of listeners seeking to deepen their understanding of the current state and possibilities for the future.

Deepening the Understanding of the Stories

Stories developed in this manner enable participants to look into the future from multiple perspectives. They encourage participants to think of possibilities without feeling the responsibilities of ownership. Stories do not have to be right; they offer opportunities to reflect on possibilities in the future. Listeners must have frames by which to understand and analyze the stories. They, too, need to overcome unconscious personal biases that may limit alternate futures.

Six Thinking Hats

Six Thinking Hats, written by Edward DeBono, describes alternate ways of perceiving a situation. DeBono's process is particularly useful in analyzing stories and their potential resolutions. Participants in the outer circle should receive a copy of Table 2-5. A facilitator from outside the group should lead.

The *Six Thinking Hats* process allows alternate views to be brought to the table. It reduces the need for hidden agendas by providing opportunities to process concerns and emotions while alter-

Table 2-5: Summary of the *Six Thinking Hats*

Hat	Symbolism	Explanation	Other Facts	Example
White	Pure facts, information	Computer, objective, neutrality. Two types: proven facts, believed truths	Spectrum of knowledge from actually true to sometimes true. Must state whether fact or philosophy	There are 150 employees in the company; I believe there are 150 employees in the company.
Red	Seething red, emotions, intuition	Emotions around the matter; makes feelings visible. Two types: emotions and judgments	No need to justify, give reasons, or be logical	I distrust him; I don't like this.
Black	Devil's advocate, critical, negative	Look for the reasons something will not work; negative assessment based on perceived risk, danger	Allows people to display negative thoughts without retribution. Often based on past experience and framed as "Yes, but..."	Will this work here? But the possibility exists that... How would you handle x, y, z.
Yellow	Possibilities, speculative	Focuses on the benefits, constructive thinking to create new alternatives, suggestions, openness	Positive assessment with the assumption that desire is a major ingredient for success. This type of thinking needs to be cultivated.	New product will do well because... There is a new way to... How can we participate?
Green	Creative, nonlinear thought	There is a solution, and it is not always logical or immediately apparent	It is difficult because of the natural inclination to rely on judgment and problem solving. Requires experimentation with no assurance of guaranteed outcome. No judgments please.	What new ways can we get people to pay attention? What would happen if we made cars half their current length? Suppose we tried it backwards? How could we get around that?
Blue	Examines how the group processes information	Think about how the group is thinking; how well is the group facilitating the meeting? How are thoughts being organized? Is the group meeting expectations?	Summarize what has taken place, establish focus, determine which hat to use, determine what might be getting in the group's way	We are arguing. Are we focused on our purpose? What might be keeping us from moving forward?

nate problem-solving approaches are explored. The process frees people to achieve a level of understanding and build commitment in a manner not typically found in strategic/tactical planning sessions.

To start your thinking imagine what might have happened if the leadership of Shopping Centers USA had employed the *Six Thinking Hats* process. During their discussions someone may have raised such questions as: Is there anything about the new mall concept that should concern us? What ideas should we adopt? What will happen to us if the new mall is successful? Certainly, Shopping Centers USA had assets that it could have used to ameliorate the situation. But the leaders did not create opportunities for alternate responses. They did not feel that exploring possibilities was necessary.

Exercise: Using the *Six Thinking Hats* to Analyze the Stories

Step 1   Select a facilitator who possesses the skill to move the group forward. This individual should be someone who doesn't have a personal stake in the outcome. The facilitator ensures that each person has a hat or a piece of paper representing each of the six thinking styles.

Step 2   Each of the groups is instructed to develop a story that includes the context, the challenge, and the resolution.

Step 3   The groups are assembled. The presenting group is in the inner circle and tells the story.

Step 4   Once the story has been told, participants in the outer circle ask questions for clarification. This ensures that the story is understood.

Step 5   The facilitator looks at the stories from each of the six styles, reserving the blue hat for those times when the group is not functioning as effectively as it should be or for when they are doing exceedingly well. As participants express their points of view, they should wear the appropriate hat.

Note: Participants may at first feel awkward trying to discern the appropriate style or remembering to hold up the appropriate hat. Within a relatively short time, these concerns dissipate.

Step 6   As dialogue about each story completes its cycle, the facilitator engages in blue-hat thinking.
- What have we learned from this story?
- What assumptions need further examination?
- What remains to be explored?
- If we were to move forward with the idea of the story, what would it mean for us?
- What are possible first steps?

Step 7   The facilitator continues with the same approach until all the stories have been told.

Creating Three Endings

Participants are asked to develop three outcomes for their stories. They create an ending that far exceeds the current reality, one in which the status quo continues, and one in which reality falls short of expectations. For example, before the construction of the Mall of America, the leaders of Shopping Centers USA might have asked:

- What will we do if the Mall of America fails?
- What will we do if Eastdale mall maintains its current revenue streams despite the Mall of America's success?
- What will we do if the Mall of America succeeds and significantly reduces Eastdale mall revenue?

Creating the three options allows leaders and employees to fully explore options. The value is not to be found in precise predictions. Rather, each of the three endings offers an early warning system for creating greater flexibility should circumstances unexpectedly change. Decision makers at Shopping Centers USA could have had an alternate plan in place when revenues faltered.

Putting the Pieces Together

At this point, participants have shared facts, emotions, and alternative courses of action. They could be overwhelmed by the complexity. They could be more knowledgeable about available options. They must now sift through the details and possibilities, and draw one or more conclusions regarding the most appropriate courses of action and their implementation. Participants are asked to develop a unified story incorporating their learning. The themes in the final story should include:

> The context
> The challenge presented to the group
> The history and process the group used to arrive at its conclusions
> The map and its S curves
> The driving forces that have concerned the participants
> The dramatic conflict:
> - What is at stake?
> - What tradeoffs must be made?
> - What if we do not succeed?
> The resolution:
> - This is the way forward. This is how we did it.
> - How did this change the lives of employees? Customers? Suppliers?
> - What new relations were formed?
> - How did the decision affect the organization's map?
> - What new capabilities ensured survival?
> - How were industry/market rules rewritten?
> - What did the organization have to give up to achieve its new positioning? What did it cost (not only financially)?
> - What did the leadership do to achieve this new result? What did they learn?

Moving from Story to Reality

The exercises described in this chapter provide an excellent opportunity to generate organizational learning and team building. They help leaders and employees become clearer about the issues and potential courses of action and their implementation. Nevertheless, the final decision to move forward generally rests with the leaders. Although the analysis, participation, and planning are extremely valuable, the decision to move forward can be lonely and emotional. If the plan succeeds, the many participants will be praised; if it does not, the leader will be left with the blame. Having the courage to focus on the long term or to do the right thing is not well understood or appreciated by those who have not shouldered leadership responsibility for an organization. The story below provides an example.

Story: Moving the Company

For most of ABC Moving Company's 60 years, it has been a premier regional household moving and storage company. Ten years ago, the growth curve for household moving reached its Phase 3 plateau. The leadership expanded its strategy first by purchasing ailing household moving companies in other parts of the country and second by offering its moving capabilities to corporations. Unfortunately, the first strategy failed. The newly acquired regional household moving companies also experienced significant margin pressures. The new corporate business was a success. ABC significantly increased revenues, which even fueled moderate growth for its household business.

Providing facility moves to corporations was a new strategy 10 years ago. Today, ABC faces similar pressures in this business. The leadership group recognized the need for yet another major shift in order to reach its desired projection of doubling growth in five years. As the participants developed the relationship map, they realized that there was a potential for a greater breadth of services that could be offered to many corporate customers. ABC could not only move furniture and equipment from one facility to another, it also could pack and ship expensive and delicate products produced by these corporate clients. The shipping of corporate products offered ABC both the potential for greater revenues and a more predictable revenue stream.

The growth potential was huge—so too was the learning curve. The shipping of products was Phase 1 on ABC's growth curve—and an unsuccessful execution placed significant revenues at risk. The participants had major concerns. They divided into three subteams and developed several scenarios. The first team projected the company's future given the assumption that it would exploit further opportunities within the existing lines of business. The second team developed a scenario given the assumption that the expanded corporate line would be offered only in one or two regions as an experiment. The third group assumed simultaneous corporate expansion for all the regions.

Each of the teams was then asked to develop stories that described the implementation of their plans. They were to fully describe the risks and opportunities, that is, to describe both the successes achieved and the travails encountered, the additional employee competencies required, the impact on financial and information systems, the requirements for additional assets, and so forth. The team charged with predicting the extension of the status quo developed the insight that if the economy were to falter, the company would be unlikely to remain independent. Reduced revenues created the potential for ABC to be swallowed by a larger moving company. The team investigating the implementation of the new strategy at a reduced pace developed insight into the high level of skill and coordination required to be successful. Uniform work processes were required; communication between regions would need to be significantly improved; the fundamental structure of each region financially operating autonomously would need to be changed. The implementation of the new corporate strategy one region at a time was not possible. The third team arrived at a similar conclusion.

The group then subjected each of the stories to the *Six Thinking Hats* exercise. Although some members had initially resisted change, this process cemented the need for it. The group was excited about the financial opportunities, but the black hat concerns encouraged frank discussion. The leaders confronted their historic inability to work effectively across regional boundaries. Uniform implementation of projects across regions was spotty. If they were going to be successful, a new approach to leadership was required. They would have to listen better to each other, support each other's weaknesses, and develop further competencies to manage the new business. The implications for headquarters functions were also significant. A new financial model would be required—one that recognized the value of sharing employees across the organization. For Human Resources, it meant the need to establish better training and compensation systems that rewarded cooperation across regional lines. The ownership of the company was asked to forego some short-term profits, and invest in the people and the required infrastructure.

The leadership group worked together to further refine the unfolding of the new corporate strategy. A new leadership structure emerged. National directors for each line of business—household and corporate—would be established and the regional leadership would be developed to ensure local success. Human Resources was charged with the responsibility of developing the corporation's leadership talent.

The leadership group then developed a communications plan. At its core was the scenario and stories developed during the planning process. Large groups of employees were brought together and asked to use the *Six Thinking Hats* as a method to deepen the knowledge of the new strategy.

The planning process encouraged participants to break away from their regional frames of reference. The shared vision was exhilarating and the agenda demanding. The resulting shared perspectives moved the leaders and employees toward cohesion. They found they had much more in common than they had initially imagined.

Summary

Having the best ideas or most sincere intentions is insufficient. The energies of many people are essential to creating a desired future. Many people must be convinced that the proposed ideas are sound, that the leadership is committed to their implementation, and that the leadership has the capacity to see the organization through to the other side. The next chapter provides tools to develop commitment.

Reframing the future is about changing fundamental business rules, creating new industries, and changing critical relationships.

To reframe the future, the leaders must understand the ecosystem in which the organization exists. One way to define the initial map is by establishing a better picture of the relationships between suppliers, customers, substitutes, and new entrants in the market.

Whether to make an evolutionary or revolutionary change often depends on where the organization is in its growth cycle. The S curve provides three stages: forming, norming, and fulfilling. The leadership challenge at each of these stages is unique. Knowing where the organization is on the curve helps leaders determine what leadership actions are required.

Discovering new approaches and means to overcome challenges often requires looking at the business in new ways. Scenario building and storytelling help participants move past their existing assumptions. Both activities encourage learning and team development.

Regardless of the extent of analysis, final decisions require leaders to listen to their intuition. Ultimately leaders need to know how they will reframe the future for their businesses and industries.

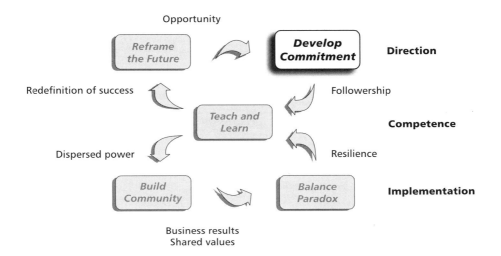

Opportunity

Reframe the Future

Develop Commitment — Direction

Redefinition of success

Followership

Teach and Learn

Competence

Dispersed power

Resilience

Build Community

Balance Paradox — Implementation

Business results
Shared values

CHAPTER 3

Develop Commitment

> If we are to continue to learn how to work together in ways that maximize responsibility and respect differences while forging unity and direction, we need to begin to notice how leadership can be something we are doing together, not the special task of a few people called leaders...
>
> —*Wilfred Drath*

The Challenge of Developing Commitment

Leadership is not a solo act. Without the commitment and support of others, dreams remain dreams and great ideas are stillborn. By addressing the challenge of reframing the future, the leader begins to create a vision of new possibilities for the organization. The principal output of that work is the articulation of new opportunities and the description of the gap that exists between where the organization is now and where it could be.

The central question of developing commitment is "Do we have the people and level of commitment we need to be successful in our work?" To see a new vision and its inherent changes come to life, leaders must gain deeper commitment from others, requiring them to act in new ways and be partners in leading the change.

What Is Followership?

Traditionally, organization leaders have thought of themselves as being in charge, able to control a situation through force of personality, pure intellect and insight, or dogged attention to detail. Such images of leaders vaguely refer to people as followers, behaving like sheep, waiting for leaders to tell them where to go and what to do. Followers, in this traditional sense, are not highly regarded.

What do superb followers look like? They share with the leader a commitment to a common purpose or goal and an understanding of their roles and responsibilities. They hold themselves and others to a common set of standards for acting and building productive relationships with others.

In truth, no leaders are smarter than everyone in their organization, and no single leader can possibly keep meaningful control of an organization. The commitment of effective followers bridges the gap between what is possible for a leader as an individual and what is possible through the aligned efforts of followers. Today, successful leaders need superb followers, not conscripts.

At its core, leadership is a process through which followers and leaders commit to accomplish the aims of an organization. If we ask respected leaders what attributes they value in followers, they will provide characteristics that sound remarkably like leadership attributes. Good followers are not sheep; they are accountable, take ownership of results, provide honest feedback, see the big picture and work toward it, and maintain a learning orientation.

We define followership as the commitment to collectively act with courage, intelligence, responsibility, and self-reliance to accomplish the organization's purpose and goals. Followership is no more a solo act than is leadership. Followership is a collective endeavor. Effective followers require the courage to transform themselves, to seek feedback, and to challenge the leader. They think critically to gain insight and to assist the leader in facing challenges. They take responsibility for results and for acting in accord with a set of personal values congruent with the team's values. Finally, they are self-reliant; they avoid unhealthy dependence on the leader.

Assessing Commitment

To answer the question, "Do I have the number of people with levels of commitment that are required to meet the challenges the organization faces?" Leaders need to take stock of the commitment of key followers.

In the beginning, a few followers will do. Every leader will sense how large a group of followers constitutes a "critical mass," which is the minimum number of people needed to sustain a change in the organization until it becomes integrated as part of the organizational life.

Numbers alone are insufficient to gain a critical mass. Equally important are the alignment and commitment needed to overcome the challenges of organization leadership. A useful tool for this task is a commitment table, based on the ideas of Richard Beckhard and Reuben Harris (1987).

Activity: Assessing the Commitment Gap

Purpose: To assess the gap between the current and the desired level of commitment needed for organizational success

Step 1   Construct a table similar to Table 3-1 and add the names of people who are critical to organizational success. Include no more than six names. They should be people you lead or can influence. You can add other names later.

Step 2   Consider their current levels of commitment to the effort you are leading, and place a "C" in the box that cor-

Table 3-1: Commitment of Key Followers

Key Followers	No Commitment	Passive Bystander	Helpful Contributor	Part of the Team	Action Plan
1. Karen			C	D	Ask her to team with Francis on Gemini project
2. James		C		D	Discuss his vision
3. Mason	C			D	
4. Claire			C	D	
5. Juanita	C			D	
6. Francis				CD	Strategize regarding other players

responds most closely to the current level of commitment.

- No commitment: They have no apparent interest in supporting your effort.
- Passive: They will not hinder progress.
- Helpful contributor: They may provide resources and other direct support to aid the effort.
- Part of the team: They will bring their full attention and resources to see the effort through to completion.

If desired, you can include additional categories in the table.

Step 3   Place a "D" in the box where you desire each of them to be.

Step 4   Consider the gap for each individual you named and develop an action plan for assisting them toward the level of commitment needed.

In assessing commitment gaps and developing action plans, consider the following questions. For each individual:

- What will it take to get real movement toward the plan?
- What level of commitment can I request?
- How can I meaningfully describe "what's in it for him or her?"
- Does what I am asking this person to do fit with his or her values and beliefs?
- What is the nature of this person's relationships with others in the group?

For the group:

- Am I willing to make the personal commitment that is necessary?
- For how long do we need their commitment? When must it start?
- What skills do we need and what skills are missing?

Addressing the Commitment Gap

Each individual will require a different approach. However, a few approaches will be useful for addressing nearly everyone. The following are examples of practical approaches, which should be designed to make significant changes, not just enhancements to the status quo:

Coaching session: To change the awareness of the followers regarding their performance, provide feedback to each individual, set improvement goals, and define what assistance you and others will provide.

Role modeling: Ensure that your words and your actions match and are congruent with the behaviors you want from your followers. Put yourself in situations in which you can demonstrate the values you want to promote and the behaviors you would like to see.

New reward structures and systems: Focus attention on the things that are critically important to the success of the effort. Remove formal and informal rewards for behaviors that do not support the new direction. Also, begin to recognize behaviors that do. Important organizational

change efforts are often fueled by first changing the reward structure of the leadership group.

Changing the workplace environment: New experiences of
the workplace change perspectives and behaviors. Reas-
signments, changing the format and the focus of meetings, and any number of other alterations signal that the
workplace is changing.

Education: Assumptions and beliefs about the way things
work can often be changed through visits to customers,
suppliers, distributors, and others.

Tension Between Leaders and Followers

Although interventions to close the commitment gap can be effective, most leaders will face issues that are made more complex because of the reality of organizational power. While power may ebb
and flow within organization divisions and among people, it is a
constant reality.

Power and authority create unavoidable tensions between
leaders and followers. While building followers' commitment to accomplish the organization's purpose and goals, leaders must inevitably deal with the needs of every individual for recognition, influence, ambition, and power. The following story illustrates this
recurring struggle:

Steven is the president and majority stockholder of a business that manufactures precision tools for the packaging
industry. He understands the technical aspects of the business inside and out, having done virtually every job in the
company. In five years, the firm has grown from startup to
$18 million annual revenues. He now dreams of growing
his business to $200 million within the next five years.
Around him, Steven has assembled a group of competent,
fast-charging managers. However, Steven can't seem to get
the managers to work together as a team. They see their
jobs as creating success in their areas. All do what they
think is best, without much regard for how their priorities
and approaches affect the other parts of the organization.

The sales organization doesn't understand the day-to-day complexity and challenges of Operations. Product Development pursues perfection in design no matter how long it takes or how expensive it gets. Manufacturing can't get product specifications ready fast enough for production. Only Steven appears to see the big picture.

Steven knows he can't possibly manage every detail of this growing company as he used to. He needs managers who will follow his lead and manage the business as a whole. Frustrated, he has begun to dive into details, solve problems, and push people to perform. As he challenges his managers to produce better results, he intensifies his interactions with each one. Their agreements seem to fall apart when the managers go off on their own, thwarting Steven's attempts to get the contributions he knows the organization needs. None of the managers openly confronts Steven when they disagree with his ideas. Rather, they find ways to do exactly what they wanted to do in the first place. Steven's team resists change. The more he attempts to impose his will, the more they dig in.

The missing elements are the accountability of managers to each other and for the success of the larger business. Steven is at a critical point in the change process. He must help them create the collaborative teamwork needed to move the company toward their five-year goal. His task is to develop commitment in his managers.

Both power and authority are at issue here. Leaders who try to wield power by imposing their will on followers only heighten resistance. Author Warren Bennis has stated that "power is the capacity to translate intention into reality and sustain it." But a sense of manipulation in the leader-follower relationship will arise whenever leaders attempt to use influence and power to get people to act.

The Impact of Power

Power differentials create a tension that makes the relationship between leader and follower paradoxical. The follower's commitment may not be to the individual leader and her ideals, but rather to his own ideals and vision of the organization. For example, a leader may be driven by her desire to build an organization, and a follower may be driven by his desire to help people. How does the leader wield her power to reconcile the difference between their commitments?

All power is not the same. Bennis describes the types of power that are commonly wielded within organizations:

> *Coercive:* Influencing through reward and punishment
> *Legitimate:* Stemming from position or tradition
> *Expert:* Associated with truth, science, and knowledge
> *Identification:* Stemming from attractiveness and charisma
> *Values:* Based on attraction to desired or common values

According to Bennis, power based on values is the most potent, and is compatible with generating commitment and resiliency in the organization. Such power is the basis for creating long-term change.

A Process for Establishing Followership

Gaining the commitment of followers goes beyond putting the "right" people in place, assembling your team, and hiring smart, capable employees. Effort and patience are also required, because establishing followership is a continuous process of deepening and strengthening the commitment of followers to act. Successful leaders actively develop followers. For followers to succeed, leaders must actively engage followers in addressing four steps:

1. Clarify purpose: Align individual purposes into a common purpose.
2. Define roles: Understand how they and others contribute to achieving the purpose.
3. Create alignment: Align words and actions through shared values and congruent behaviors.
4. Build relationships: Sustain healthy working relationships based on trust.

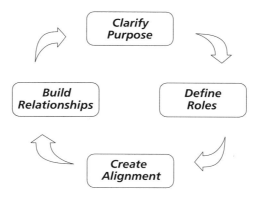

Figure 3-1: A Process for Establishing Commitment

We will describe each of the steps and their accompanying is-sues in detail and provide you with tools to successfully address each step.

The sequence for addressing the four steps described in Figure 3-1 is based on the following assumptions:

- The commitment of followers is built on solid relationships based on trust, but such relationships are difficult to create and maintain without addressing the other three steps.
- A common *purpose* for the endeavor must be expressed before roles can be defined and agreed to.
- *Roles* must be defined and agreed to before the group can de-fine the rules and values they will employ for working to-gether, which builds alignment.
- When there is a lack of alignment or little common agree-ment on how to work together, relationships suffer.
- Without relationships built on trust, people cannot begin to have honest discussion about common purpose.

These assumptions suggest a hierarchy for addressing issues. When leaders don't know and understand the appropriate sequence, they may have people charging off in all different directions.

The Process Applied to Steven's Dilemma

Earlier, we related Steven's inability to establish effective follower-ship. The lack of alignment, differing interpretations of roles, and unclear purpose confused the members of the management team. Conflict was not addressed constructively; no one confronted Steven when they disagreed with him. Lack of trust strained relationships and jeopardized the organization's future. How did the situation evolve to such a state?

Steven focused on individuals and met face-to-face with them to state his expectations for their roles and how they would work together. He locked into the role of directing traffic for the management team rather than engaging them collectively in the larger issue of understanding where they and the organization were going. As a result, Steven has work to do that will involve taking the lead in building trust within the management team. Once the air has cleared and the issue of trust has been constructively dealt with, Steven will have a stronger basis on which to lead the group in defining a common purpose.

The organization's circumstances will help the leader decide where to begin, but the commitment of followers will not be fully established until all tasks have been addressed. A leader may, for example, believe that sufficient trust is present in a situation or that trust is not the central issue. She may believe that a shift of purpose has caused people to lose track of what is important to the whole organization. In this case, the leader's task is to help followers understand the new organizational direction and redefine their roles to meet a specific new purpose.

How the Process Addresses Conflict

There is a human tendency to attribute workplace conflict to personality clashes, poor relationships, personal motives, and ultimately to a fundamental lack of trust. Much conflict, however, is embedded within the context of the work in which the group is engaged. Take, for example, a typical work team. When tensions rise and ill feelings surface, the leader, rather than immediately zeroing in on issues of lack of trust, will find it worthwhile to ask whether the team is aligned around a common set of standards about how they will work together. The remedy might be as simple as creating ground rules or as complex as gaining agreement between functions about how certain business issues will be handled.

But ground rules can be ignored and agreements can fall through. Common standards cannot easily be created unless the people creating them are clear about their own roles. Do they know how others expect them to contribute? Until roles are defined, people tend to create their roles as they work, which will lead to conflicts.

Finally, neither common standards nor role clarity can make up for an unclear purpose. Without an agreement about where the group intends to go and what they wish to accomplish, individual agendas will always clash. Personal agendas are not necessarily negative; they are a normal response to unclear purpose. Nevertheless, personal agendas can threaten the trust level of a group.

Activity: Determining Where to Focus

Purpose: To diagnose what is going on in your circle of influence and determine which of the four sequential steps to focus on

Step 1   Identify key followers.

Step 2   Ask yourself the following questions about them:
- Do they disagree about how to coordinate or do the work?
- Do they disagree about setting priorities in the work?
- Are their interactions honest, civil, and candid?

If the answer to *all* the questions is YES, focus on creating alignment. If the answer to any question is NO, go to the next step.

Step 3   Ask yourself the following questions:
- Are people unclear about what they are expected to do?
- Do people have unrealistic expectations of each other?
- Are interactions between people honest, civil, and candid?

If the answer to *all* the questions is YES, focus on defining roles. If the answer to any question is NO, go to the next step.

Step 4   Ask yourself the following questions:
- Do people differ on the overall purpose of their work?
- Do people disagree on the most important outcome of their work together?
- Are the interactions between people honest, civil, and candid?

If the answer to *all* the questions is YES, focus on clarifying the purpose. If the answer to any question is NO, go to the next step.

Step 5   Ask yourself the following questions:
- Are the interactions between people defensive, recriminating, or cynical?
- Should people "clear the air" about what has happened?

If the answer to *either* of these questions is YES, focus on building relationships.

Tips:
- The presence of conflict does not indicate the need to focus on building trust. Resolving other issues first may be sufficient.
- If responses to any of the questions are not a clear yes or no, move "upstream" to the next step.

Clarify Purpose

One dynamic tension of followership is that followers can choose not to follow. Author Gary Wills has said, "It is not the noblest call that gets answered, but the answerable call." (Wills, 1994) The leader who desires the commitment of followers will create the "answerable call," which is a clear statement of direction and purpose—a practical and appealing message.

In Chapter 2, "Reframe the Future," you identified an opportunity for your organization. In this chapter, we challenge you to communicate the organization's purpose, to make it real for others. At this stage in your leadership journey, it is important to be clear about organizational purpose and to clarify your personal purpose to help gain the commitment of followers.

Personal Purpose

Your personal purpose answers the question, "Why are you here as a leader, and what do you wish to create?" Regardless of size, an organization will always be helped by a leader with a clear sense of personal purpose and vision. The work of bringing clarity and focus to purpose and vision has great value. This work, if left undone, will show up as conflict with and between followers around roles and rules.

The astonishing pace of change in today's business environment may seem to obviate the value of clarity of purpose. The opposite is true. In an uncertain environment, the importance of purpose is amplified. Given daily, weekly, and monthly changes and challenges, a clear purpose informs minute-to-minute decisions.

Activity: Defining Your Personal Purpose

Purpose: To define your personal purpose

Step 1   In a quiet place where you can spend a few uninterrupted moments, consider the following scenario:

It is 10 years into the future, and you are just arriving at the reunion of a successful team that you led in a time of great accomplishment, personal growth, and organizational success. Being their leader was not easy. It was simultaneously the most challenging and the most rewarding work you had done up to that point. Later you moved on to other career challenges.

You are a little late arriving, and the group has begun to reminisce about their time of great challenge and accomplishment. They are talking about the kind of leader you were and what made it all work so well. Each person talks about the lasting effect you had on them and the organization.

Step 2   Reflect and record your thoughts about the following:

- What are people saying about the lasting effect you had on them and the organization?
- What key leadership behaviors and practices supported the lasting effects they mentioned?
- What were you passionate about then?
- Why were your passions important to you and to others?

Step 3   Review your notes and look for themes.
- How would you describe your personal purpose?
- Can your personal purpose find expression today through the purpose of your organization?
- How does your personal purpose fit with the purposes of each of your followers?

Step 4   List the key themes and carry the list with you for a few days.
- Share your list with a trusted colleague or two.
- Write your personal purpose and live with it for a while longer.

You are ready to weave your personal purpose into stories that can powerfully illustrate your purpose.

Get Personal

Creating an environment where all are engaged in building trust begins when the leader models trust. Bringing "who you are" to work means first to be willing to talk about what is important to you and why and second to actively encourage and listen to others as they do the same.

Everyone's work life has a public and a private side. Bringing "who you are" to your work carries with it some risk because it involves self-disclosure. Some people are comfortable disclosing much more than others. It is important to respect your own and others' privacy, and if you find yourself never venturing beyond your comfort zone, you may assume that others will remain equally guarded.

Everybody has stories about people, places, and events of importance in their lives. Conventional wisdom tells us that in human interactions, people most often remember the stories. Telling stories (real or plausible) is essential to leaving lasting impressions. Stories represent what you are striving to communicate. They connect people on a personal level because they appeal to both their rational and their emotional nature.

A toy company executive used a personal story to reveal one of the driving forces in his work to produce outstanding toys for young children. He recalls how, as an only child, he loved to create things that he could use to entertain himself. He immersed himself in toy catalogs, studied the advertisements at the back of comic books, and saved his allowance to purchase toys and gadgets. One day he spent his savings on a model ship and worked intensely to assemble and paint it. When his father arrived home and saw the model, he berated his son for wasting his money on a useless thing. The boy felt crushed and carried that moment with him into adulthood. He decided he would make toys that were worthy of children's dreams and fantasies and the respect and approval of their parents. The executive tells his story as a personal testament to childhood pain and to his commitment to enhancing the lives and experiences of children.

Telling stories is an effective way to communicate to followers what is important to you. Stories let others tap into the energy you bring to the organization. Stories beget more stories. Their telling gives others personal insight to your level of commitment and personal purpose.

Noel Tichy, advisor and consultant to business leaders, has written about the need to develop others through a "teachable point of view." The following exercise, which is derived from his approach, describes a systematic way to create your own story profile.

Developing a Story Profile: A Tool for Generating Stories

Purpose:
- Demonstrate self-disclosure by communicating incidents that shaped you and your values
- Create consistency between who you are and what you hope to see the organization achieve

Step 1   Reflect on and record:
- The pivotal events in your life; events that shaped your perspective of the world and what you believe.
- The most influential individuals in your life, and why.
- Your most significant learning experiences; both successes and failures.

Step 2   Reflect on and record the values that you most wish the organization to stand for today.

Step 3   Choose a past experience from Step 1 that matches with a value or values you identified in Step 2.
- Record it on one page; include as many specific details as you can.
- From the details, craft a brief story with a clear point.

Step 4   Test your story on a few trusted associates or friends. Request feedback about its impact, clarity, and relevance.

Step 5   Communicate the story to a larger audience and continue to request feedback.

Tips: • Keep your story brief.
- Be sure it has a clear point.
- Remember, the purpose is not to entertain, but to focus attention and communicate your values in a compelling way.
- The story must be absolutely true.
- You must act in a manner consistent with the values you express in the story; hypocrisy will have a devastating effect.
- Humor is appropriate, but your story will be most compelling if you express personal vulnerability and simple humanity.

Telling stories is a simple and powerful way to express what you value and why you think and act the way you do. When you begin to share your stories on a human level, others will too. Learn to read the reactions of your audience, and watch for signs that they have a clearer sense of your values, purpose, and behavior.

Defining Roles: Knowing How Leaders and Others Contribute

Knowing where an organization is going is critical to making progress. However, without the definition of individual and collective roles and expectations, progress toward goals will be limited, and personal conflict will result.

Because followers and leaders depend on one another for their mutual success, a discussion of leadership cannot go very far without considering what followers and leaders offer each other. In situations characterized by change, normal communication practices will not be adequate or even appropriate. The leader must establish communication about roles and responsibilities of key followers.

Kenneth Keller, the former president of the University of Minnesota, led the University to examine its mission of teaching, research, and service. The effort, which he called "A Commitment to Focus," was aimed at sharpening the broad mandate of the University, eliminating marginal programs, and consolidating resources in areas of excellence. His efforts were controversial and accompanied by conflict and active resistance among faculty and staff. A few departments would be closed, others would be expanded. As money became exceedingly tight and greater fiscal restraint became inevitable, the proposed changes threatened the livelihoods of many people. But Keller remained confident, and his vision was compelling.

In the midst of the change effort, reports surfaced that Keller had authorized an extensive remodeling of the president's residence, which was owned by the University and had been inhabited by successive presidents for the better part of the last century. Keller was accused of feathering his own nest while faculty faced cutbacks and potential loss of their jobs. The controversy grew and was played out in the local media. It ended after Keller resigned and was replaced by another, who we were assured was as honest as the day is long.

The ideas Keller introduced continued to provide the blueprint for change. They influence the thinking of University planners to this day. Nevertheless, Keller's leadership skills were lost to the University. Was he a poor leader? No. He had many capable followers, but none could help him see the obvious contradiction between his personal and public actions. He had failed to develop followers who could help him work through all the challenges he faced as a leader. Keller was not perfect, but, expecting perfection, followers did not challenge him to improve his leadership. The result was the loss of a unique leadership capability that could have been preserved if Keller had developed followers with well-defined roles and responsibilities.

Many followers hold their leaders to a high standard. Expectations that they will be perfect can isolate leaders and push them into a remote and inaccessible position. High expectations can also create a constant tension, under which followers rarely acknowledge the contributions of their leaders, and leaders seldom recognize the good performers around them. Leaders need followers who will not treat them as if they were perfect. Moreover, they need followers who will challenge them when they lose touch with reality. You've heard people say, "When you're promoted, that's the last day you hear the truth."

Formal and Informal Roles

Every organization has formal roles, which are defined primarily by the work and the environment in which the organization operates. Formal roles are often identified through job titles and descriptions, organizational charts, and performance management systems. It is essential that formal roles be defined, but they are not the focus of this chapter on followership.

Informal Roles

We focus on informal roles because they are often neglected in discussions of leadership. Informal roles are based on expectations. The following are examples of informal roles that develop between leaders and followers.

> *Initiator:* Takes ideas and gets things started—is good at seeing opportunity and taking action

Confidant: Listens and supports the leader and followers—allows private thoughts to surface and be acknowledged

Impartial observer: Helps the leader and followers weigh the pros and cons of various actions—does not introduce significant personal bias

Pulse taker: Gives the leadership team feedback—accesses areas of the corporation where the signal is weak

Truth teller: Tells the truth even when the message is not popular—tells you when you have no clothes on

Seer: Sees into areas of organizational life where you have limited vision—brings to the surface indicators of significant disturbances in the organization

Kindred spirit: Shares the same dream—knows what makes the team tick and is dedicated to success

These informal roles are often the first indications of emerging leadership. For example, for Kenneth Keller individuals filling these informal roles could have been pivotal in providing the kind of support necessary for his long-term success. Keller needed a truth teller to awaken him to the dangers of spending scarce dollars for what appeared to be personal gain. Informal roles deserve thoughtful consideration on the part of leaders and followers.

Consider the examples in Table 3-2 of what leaders and followers might expect from one another.

Activity: A Tool for Identifying Informal Roles and Expectations

Purpose: Identify informal roles and expectations between a leader and a group of followers

Step 1   Set up a chart like the one shown in Table 3–2. In the right-hand column, list what you expect of the people with whom you work closely.

Step 2   In the left-hand column, list what they expect of you.

Step 3   Identify glaring inconsistencies or gaps. It may be helpful to refer to Table 1 in the Introduction, where you

Table 3-2: What Leaders and Followers Expect

What Followers Expect from Leaders	What Leaders Expect from Followers
Integrity	Best work
Direction/vision	Honesty—good and bad news
Follow-through	Persistence
Respect	Independence
Energy	Loyalty/team player
Consistency between word and deed	Take risks/learn from mistakes
Courage	Accountability for results
	Participation
	Commitment to the success of the organization

listed the perceptions people had of you as a leader and added your own self-assessment.

Step 4   Rate how well you think you are fulfilling others' expectations of you, and vice versa. Use a scale: 1 = seldom, 2 = sometimes, 3 = almost always.

Step 5   Consider the following questions:
   • Are people clear about your expectations of them?
   • Are you clear about their expectations of you?
   • How will your followers know if they are not fulfilling your expectations?

Step 6   Identify your key followers from the Commitment Table (Table 3-1) and begin to define both their formal and informal organizational roles.

Step 7   Meet with each of your key followers and define the informal roles they expect to play.

Create Alignment

Once you have begun to clarify roles, it is important to establish alignment among leaders and followers. One essential ingredient is a set of rules for working together. For example, when Lance, a new plant manager, began his work at the plant by taking the first two weeks to walk around and talk to everybody, he was not only redefining the role of plant manager, he was also changing the communication rules in the workplace. He was extending permission to talk to management about problems.

Changing the rules can be a powerful symbol of other changes in the organization. Loren Ames, President of INCO Manitoba, decided that the daily inspections of workers as they left the plant did not communicate the cooperative and respectful working environment he felt was needed. He stopped the long-standing practice of inspection, which had been designed to ensure that workers did not steal tools or nickel. The message in this change in rules was immediate and powerful, far beyond that of any formal communication. Workers took careful note. For a while Ames enjoyed a unique opportunity to align people behind new ways of working together.

Often, there exists a mismatch between workplace practices and espoused values and rules. In Chapter 2 in the Shopping Centers USA example, people were encouraged to be entrepreneurial and to act as if they owned the business, but whenever they made changes they got their wings clipped. The alignment of a leader's words and deeds and the diffusion of a common set of rules and values in the workplace differentiate between good and bad places to work. Creating alignment is one of the most difficult and most important jobs of the leader.

Although, the leader can change the values and related behaviors that the organization will live by, it is difficult to change people who do not share the same values. Jim Collins, who has written extensively about leadership, claims that the leader who overmanages is making up for a mismatch in values between person and organization during the hiring process.

A useful way to think about values and rules is to discover what a few of the biggest barriers to success are in the organization and look at the practices that accompany them. Changing the rules in the workplace can begin to shift a few of the practices and remove a few of the barriers.

Behind every workplace rule lies one or more fundamental beliefs. If a leader believes in the dignity of human beings, workplace practices and rules should reflect that belief. Loren Ames understood that gate inspections reflected an underlying assumption that the workers were dishonest. This practice did not represent his belief about people. He desired to base his relationships with key followers on the premise that they were honest. Changing the rule made it possible for his leadership to emerge.

Activity: Establishing Rules

Purpose: To articulate the essential rules for creating workplace conditions that are optimal for success.

Step 1   List a few of the barriers and practices that are unproductive in your organization. Look for places where the organization sends mixed messages. For example, do leaders encourage creativity, but does everyone freely criticize new ideas?

Step 2   Share your lists with your followers and identify the barriers that if removed would make working together more productive.

Step 3   Identify the belief system that will be changed by changing a rule.

Step 4   Write rules that address barriers and narrow the list of rules to no more than five.

Step 5   Ask others in the organization to reflect on the five rules and the values that seem to underlie them.

Building Relationships: Ground Zero for Developing Commitment Among Followers

At the core of leadership are the relationships leaders build with followers and the relationships followers have with each other. Relationships are at the foundation of a leader's work. The four steps provide a framework for systematically strengthening relationships with followers. Addressing the four steps will often build trust. There are times, however, when trust is so absent that no meaningful dialogue on purpose, roles, and alignment can occur. Building trust is an intangible, personal challenge and an ongoing leadership issue.

The regard for others that the leader brings to key relationships is critical to developing the commitment of followers. While the first three steps are concerned with "What you are doing." Building trust is ultimately connected to "Who you are being." In the final analysis, who you are carries the day.

Build Trust: Sustaining Healthy Working Relationships

Brian is in a leadership position, and he sincerely wants to lead. Although he has many of the qualities of a leader—he is visionary, intelligent, courageous, positive, and energetic—he is also perceived as a hatchet man, hasty to act, not to be trusted, and willing to trade the careers of others for his own.

Which set of characteristics is true? Both are. Brian has the potential to be an excellent leader, but a few skeletons remain in his closet. Through feedback and significant effort, he has been trying to rid himself of the labels and judgments of his past. He has struggled to relearn a few skills. Brian has quickly assessed situations and taken action. However, his actions, while courageous, were short-sighted and resulted in effects that he did not foresee.

Today, Brian takes great care to involve others in helping to assess situations and evaluate alternate actions. He has begun to gain the commitment of key individuals to work collaboratively with him and provide leadership for his area. Brian has undertaken a great deal of soul searching and much trial-and-error learning. He has had to recover from his errors, endure the words of his critics, and bear the scorn of those who thought he could not change. He has changed.

Brian understood that the most critical task before him was to regain trust. He knew he must set out to build trust, for without it, his actions, even if they were intelligent and appropriate, would be regarded with suspicion.

About Trust in Relationships

Trusting relationships are indispensable in any collective human endeavor. Trust enormously affects our ability to work together. Without trust almost nothing of lasting value can happen, and what *does* happen will never come easily. Where trust is missing, simple misunderstandings will be blown out of proportion, well-considered plans will fail, and discussions will become abrasive and defensive.

Defining trust is like defining art. Views of trust are inherently subjective. People may have difficulty describing trust, but "they know it when they see it." We can agree with someone but still not trust him; we can disagree with others but nevertheless trust them. In the end, gaining trust simply requires being trustworthy, but people naturally differ on what they value as being worthy of trust. Stephen Covey suggests that being worthy of trust is based on two things:

- Character, or who you are as a person
- Competence, or what you can do

Competence relates to the leader's capacity to follow through and accomplish the things she said she was going to do. It is about credibility. Character, on the other hand, is about who the leader is and how she shows her concern for others. It is about the respect and empathy she shows for others' circumstances and perspectives, especially in times of great stress. The leader cannot work closely with others if she cannot consistently demonstrate her concern and respect for them day in and day out.

In the final analysis, we are most likely to build trust when we temporarily put aside our endless rational discussions about what people know or don't know, and instead try to understand why people value the things they do. In the next chapter, "Teach and Learn," we suggest several approaches and provide tools to improve one's ability to build trust.

Building Trust Through Listening and Empathy

Organizations bring out the best and worst in people. Samuel Culbert and John McDonough, authors of several books on the role of trust in organizations, contend that trusting relationships are the "most efficient management tool ever invented." They caution that every situation has inherent political forces that must be recognized and dealt with, and they state that communication skills and empathy are indispensable to building trust.

Sometimes the oldest tools are the best tools. By far the most effective practice for building trust is listening fully to what others want to express. Active listening must be carefully cultivated as a skill and consciously employed as a discipline whenever conflict arises and wherever it is necessary to deal with sensitive issues. Listening is "active" when it requires fully concentrating on the speaker, the speaker's words, and the speaker's intended meanings. The active listener is intensively involved, demonstrates empathy by accepting the other person's statements of feelings, and focuses on the underlying meaning of what is being said.

Taking Stock

The four steps of developing commitment suggest a repeating cycle. The leader can expect to work through the steps again and again as followers come and go through many changes in direction. Use the Followership Progress Table as a means for recording your continuing journey to develop commitment of your followers.

Activity: Followership Progress Table

Purpose: To record the status of a leader's development using the Develop Commitment process

Step 1   List the names of your key followers in Table 3-3.

Step 2   Assess the status of your relationships with your followers using the following criteria:

Table 3-3: Followership Progress

Name	Purpose	Roles	Alignment	Relationships	Actions
Claire	1	2	3	2	Get better clarity around her role
Francis	1	1	2	2	Discuss expectations on teamwork
Jackson	3	3	3	2	Figure out how to get him on board

1. Very clearly defined with common agreement
2. Somewhat defined with no agreement
3. Not defined and no agreement

Step 3   Define the actions you will take to strengthen your followership. To help define several of the actions, look at the Followership Practices Table (Table 3-4).

Followership Practices Table

Table 3-4 can be used to identify behaviors that will strengthen commitment in the organization and to assess whether followership practices can be discerned in the organization.

Summary

Developing commitment is a deeply personal challenge for every leader and his or her followers. In the end the leader must ask, "Do I have the people and the levels of commitment that I need to lead? Do we have the bench strength to move this effort forward?"

Table 3-4: Followership Practices

Establish Commitment Practices	*Purpose*	*Role*	*Alignment*	*Relationship*
Share customer's experiences with employees	✓			
Celebrate others' accomplishments	✓			✓
Weave high-level goals into all communication	✓			
Develop/tell stories regarding personal history and vision	✓	✓	✓	✓
Develop/tell stories regarding company history and vision	✓		✓	✓
Choose your three most important values and determine how you will live them			✓	✓
Define your role as leader, share, and seek further input		✓	✓	✓
In each encounter, treat each person as if he or she mattered				✓
Demonstrate the connections between division/individual objectives and mission/vision of organization		✓	✓	
Establish mutually agreed upon expectations		✓	✓	✓
Circulate among employees	✓		✓	✓
Create strong alliances inside and out of the organization		✓	✓	✓
Listen to criticism and change your behavior as necessary		✓		✓
Be decisive when it is appropriate		✓	✓	✓
Choose a leader when it is appropriate for you to follow		✓	✓	
Choose the right people for the right jobs		✓		
Surface and resolve conflict		✓	✓	
Welcome diversity of thought, gender, etc.			✓	✓
Listen to the voices of others		✓	✓	✓
Ask for suggestions and implement as appropriate		✓	✓	✓
Fully think through a proposed course of action before implementing it			✓	
Plan for presentations, meetings, and personal interactions rather than rely on capability to act extemporaneously, i.e., know what you want		✓		✓
Remove underperforming people when they have not responded to coaching. Do so in a manner that maintains their integrity		✓		
Provide honest, ongoing feedback		✓	✓	✓
Keep your promises		✓		
Groom others so they can become future leaders			✓	
Allow others to contribute to the manner in which the organization operates		✓	✓	✓
When appropriate, create "space" for people to determine how they will contribute		✓		
Explain your intentions/actions			✓	
Teach others to be open/honest in relationships with each other			✓	✓

There are four steps that a leader and followers can take to improve the chances of success in creating a critical leadership mass:

1. Clarify personal purpose
2. Define roles and responsibilities
3. Create alignment around rules for working together
4. Establish relationships that transcend day-to-day relationships in the workplace.

In the next chapter, "Teach and Learn," the leader and followers will test their commitment and alignment, and further develop their capacity to articulate ideas and learn from their interactions with employees, customers, and other stakeholders. The test could come in different forms. It could come internally from interactions with followers and follower groups. It could come from the outside from shareholders or the investment community. Ultimately, important stakeholders will assess their confidence in the organization's leadership group.

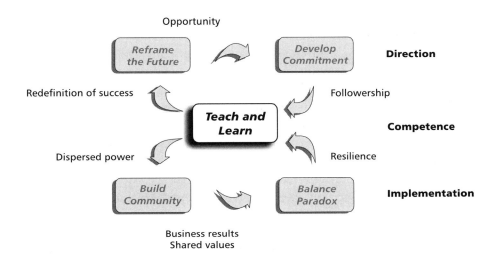

Opportunity

Reframe the Future

Develop Commitment

Direction

Redefinition of success

Teach and Learn

Followership

Competence

Dispersed power

Resilience

Build Community

Balance Paradox

Implementation

Business results
Shared values

CHAPTER 4

Teach and Learn

The culture shifts when the conversation shifts.

—*Peter Block*

The Challenge of Teaching and Learning

At the center of the Leader's Map is "Teach and Learn," the engine that provides the power, momentum, and insight for addressing the other four challenges. Recall that in Chapter 3, "Develop Commitment," you created commitment to implement the changes that your organization must undergo. In this chapter, "Teach and Learn," the leadership task is to increase not only people's competence, but also their confidence, to carry out the new direction.

The power to adapt and to act must be generated and distributed throughout the organization. This power fuels the shared capacity of the people in the organization to learn and to use that learning for their benefit and for the benefit of their organization. Simply put, teaching and learning infuses a contagious energy into the organization. It is essential to meeting the next challenge—building community. Without teaching and learning, an organization can get locked into patterns of behavior that will hasten its decline.

Learning can be defined as the individual and collective ability of people to reflect on past behavior, identify alternatives, and change how they act. Competence is the work-related knowledge and skill that currently exists within the organization. For learning to occur, however, more than competence is required. Confidence is required to overcome the fears of challenging assumptions and trying out new behaviors. People may have knowledge, but the forces that stop them from applying it, sharing it, and building on it typically are not rational. They are emotional, social, and cultural. These forces conspire to inhibit learning. For example, the emotional need for power or recognition leads to hoarding knowledge. The fear of retribution prevents people from "telling it like it is." And the desire for security blinds people from seeing hard truths.

Issues of courage and risk-taking are also related to confidence. To use an analogy, we need only recall that gaining competence in swimming—learning to breathe and to tread water—was something quite apart from acquiring the confidence to overcome our fear of being in water over our heads. Although we may have experienced these learning challenges differently, we had to accomplish both before we could truly say we had learned how to swim.

Today, success in generating organizational change is more than ever dependent on learning. When the required competence and confidence to learn are missing, an organization can be said to have a poor learning climate. It could be filled with individuals who assume that the need to learn stopped with high school or college graduation.

The social context of an organization adds a layer of complexity to learning. Pride, fear, and unhealthy competition impede learning. Pride and fear are personal to the individual. Unhealthy

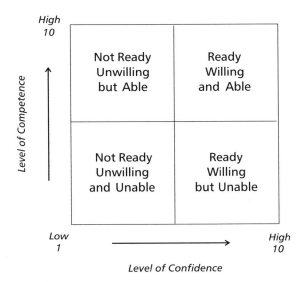

Figure 4-1: Learning Climate Matrix

competition is structural. Competitive structures are often set up by managers who believe that directly competing individuals or groups produce better work. Unfortunately, unhealthy competition slows productivity and inhibits creativity as people attend more to their competitors than to their work.

    The matrix in Figure 4-1 synthesizes the relationship between competence and confidence and teaching and learning. In the presence of a relatively high level of competence and confidence, an individual, a group, or an organization is ready, willing, and able to learn. Within the matrix, readiness and willingness equal motivation to learn. Ability is the competence that can be applied to learning.

Competence/Confidence: A Tool for Evaluating a Learning Climate

Purpose: To provide a baseline perspective for determining what actions will be needed to improve the ability of the organization to learn and adapt

Step 1   Define a specific issue or problem that will require the organization to fundamentally change (perhaps one related to an opportunity discovered in redefine the map).

Step 2   For each function or group, use a scale of 1 to 10 to assess the level of competence that people have to address the issue successfully.

Step 3   For each function or group, use a scale of 1 to 10 to assess the level of confidence that people have to address the issue successfully.

Step 4   Place the name of the function or group in the appropriate location on the matrix.

Step 5   Determine a strategy for improving the learning climate in the group and in the organization as a whole.

Tips: • The matrix yields a subjective diagnosis. It presents a starting point in exploring an organization's learning climate.
   • Other leaders can assess the same group and compare their findings.
   • Apply this matrix to diagnose your own readiness to learn.

As the matrix demonstrates, the first step in addressing the challenge of teaching and learning is to understand and come to grips with the learning climate in the organization. Only then can the leader structure priorities and leverage time for maximum impact on the organization. See the completed matrix in Figure 4-2.

The example in Figure 4-2 describes an organization in which the functions possess varying levels of competence and confidence. Human Resources is perceived to have the confidence and the desire to challenge prevailing assumptions and the corresponding competence to do so. Product Development and Finance, on the other hand, have relatively high levels of competence, but both lack the confidence and the desire to apply it. Manufacturing's learning climate lags the rest of the organization. Leadership action is required to address not only what manufacturing needs to learn but also to assess its readiness and willingness to take on new behaviors.

Figure 4-2: Learning Climate Matrix Example

In summary, followers pay very careful attention to their leader's actions. The Teach and Learn challenge puts the leader's learning behavior under a microscope. Leaders need to help people learn how to learn, how to learn faster, and, especially, how to learn together. The positive spirit they bring to this challenge, their capacities to engage with other people, and their courage to let themselves be vulnerable are critical components of success in learning. As they become proficient at the Teach and Learn challenge, leaders will unleash the full power of the organization to accomplish its goals. The following example depicts how one leader began to do that.

Teaching and Learning in a Refinery

The huge refinery was 16 months into the "big change effort." Daryl, the director of maintenance, wondered if any kind of real change was possible in this century-old sprawling complex of tanks, pipelines, and steam. Yes, evidence of the "big change effort" was tangible. Teams met regularly. A series of large group-awareness sessions had been completed. And the newsletter was full of stories about training. Daryl had seen such efforts before, and he was discouraged. He wasn't really a cynical person, but he couldn't see how all of this activity would really have an impact on the future of the struggling refinery. He knew how important his managerial role in this effort could be, but he struggled to understand what he should be doing on a daily basis. He lacked a role model.

Then Lorne, the new General Manager, arrived, and took the refinery by storm. He was pragmatic, quick, and tireless. He quickly sensed the fragmentation, alienation, and fear that gripped the organization. During the first two weeks, he hardly set foot in his office. He visited every corner of the operation. He asked operators to walk him through their work areas. He listened to technicians express their frustrations with the control system. He asked the financial group to describe the challenges they faced in gathering and analyzing refinery performance data. Some people privately questioned the value of these activities; they wondered why Lorne didn't focus on the bigger picture. But Lorne very deliberately deployed his interests in the organization by teaching and learning. He freely acknowledged that he learned as he listened. He took what he learned in one area and shared it in another, always acknowledging the names of his teachers. He often heard the concerns of a few and willingly gave them broader expression.

Daryl witnessed how Lorne's actions influenced people in the refinery and the ways they responded. People became reenergized. The fear and uncertainty that had paralyzed the organization began to dissolve. The positive effects of Lorne's actions were not lost on Daryl. He began to do things differently. He replaced his large office desk with a small one, which he placed in the corner. He regularly gathered staff around a large round table to talk, listen, and explore concerns. Issues that previously had been unexpressed began to surface. Change in the working environment of the maintenance area became tangible.

The Leader's Role

Almost any experienced teacher will say that teaching others is impossible without their willingness to learn. Many teachers also will say that the more they teach, the more they learn.

Was Lorne teaching or was he learning? If you were to ask him, he might have replied, "both." Distinguishing between teaching and learning is probably not worth the effort. The distinction is not important. The value of both showed in the effects of his actions on individuals and functional groups in the refinery. Lorne began his work at the refinery by creating an atmosphere for free and candid interactions. He demonstrated his willingness to listen and learn. As he engaged people face to face, he expressed his values and his perspective. The effect was to give others the freedom and the confidence to do the same.

The leader's role in addressing the Teach and Learn challenge includes helping people develop competence and confidence in three dimensions:

Interpersonal: The ability to cooperate and share learning
Organizational: The ability to understand and shape how the
    organization works
Technical: The ability to fulfill the leadership role in the orga-
    nization

These dimensions are interrelated. Leaders have considerable influence in shaping growth in each of them, but their greatest influence will be felt in helping people develop competencies in the interpersonal dimension.

Interpersonal Learning

Within the context of the Leader's Map, we have so far talked about the need to work with other leaders to redefine the map and develop followership. Like other challenges, the challenge to teach and learn is not a solo act.

Demonstrate Learning

The first, and perhaps most important, principle for addressing the challenge to teach and learn is to stop worrying about teaching and start demonstrating learning. This may be discomforting. Most leaders feel the pressure to provide answers, not to ask more questions. But providing answers has little to do with teaching, and even less to do with learning. The principle of demonstrating learning has far more to do with displaying new behaviors than with creating training plans, preserving "intellectual capital," or improving technical competence. Not that those things aren't important. The power of leadership by example is probably the single most important influence on whether or not an organization is a safe place for learning and for accepting the inevitable mistakes that accompany true learning.

Lorne visibly practiced what he wanted to see, a more open and adaptable organization. Daryl adopted a similar approach, not because Lorne suggested it, but because he saw the effect of Lorne's actions. Learning is led, not managed. The leader's actions speak louder than words.

Demonstrate learning, and you will be teaching. No matter how eloquently a leader may champion the value of learning, associates will believe it only when they see her personally wrestling with and acting on new learning. Despite the widespread (and mistaken) belief in the corporate world that once people have a rational understanding of what is to be done, they will act accordingly, many change efforts have ground to a halt over the past decade. Knowing doesn't necessarily lead to doing. Training doesn't guarantee a change in work performance.

Emotional Intelligence

The reasons why people act or don't act go beyond the rational; they are also social and emotional. Daniel Goleman has written about the need for leaders (and others) to possess and cultivate "emotional intelligence," an individual's capacity for self-awareness, self-control, persistence, motivation, empathy, and social skills. Emotional intelligence, defined in these terms, is much more useful than pure intellect in the pursuit of learning. The energetic, self-assured person who communicates effectively with others will contribute more to the expansion of everybody's learning than the brilliant loner who alienates others.

The interpersonal dimension is closely tied to emotional intelligence. People often fail to act because they are insufficiently motivated or because they fear the consequences of their actions. For example, virtually everyone will say that receiving personal feedback is a perfectly rational and appropriate way to learn. But how many of us avoid asking others for feedback because it may be discomforting? Few leaders like feeling vulnerable. We would rather not face our weaknesses. Social and emotional forces are magnified when the organization is in the throes of great change. Leaders have considerable influence in shaping the way the organization nurtures the emotional intelligence of its people, and they can have an enormous impact on the capacity of individuals to overcome these forces.

Probably no skill is more important to learning than the ability to gather accurate and honest feedback about one's impact on others and one's effectiveness as a leader. The leader cannot improve without it. The task is complicated by the fact that most people hide their true feelings because of the power and influence they perceive the leader to have over their well-being. In organizations where people are not likely to provide direct feedback to each other for fear of retribution, they are less likely to provide feedback to leaders. Thus, to acquire honest feedback requires courage, creativity, and perseverance. Overcoming the fear of giving and receiving feedback takes time and patience. To elicit feedback from others, the leader must communicate a willingness to be vulnerable, to take criticism. This is the essential first step to creating a learning environment.

The leader who wishes to take that step can use the following tool as a guide to determine the most appropriate method for eliciting feedback from associates.

Eliciting Feedback: a Collection of Methods

Purpose: To create a climate where people feel safe enough to provide candid, constructive feedback to one another. Table 4-1 shows methods by which leaders elicit feedback.

Table 4-1: Methods by Which Leaders Elicit Feedback

Method of Feedback	*When to Use the Method*	*Specific Tips*
One-on-One and Direct Methods		
Written Response	When the person's preferred style of communication is writing When the person does not feel threatened about giving direct feedback	Feedback posed as suggestions rather than as negative feelings is less threatening. Agree on the level of detail and how and when feedback will be shared. Give the person the option of a face-to-face meeting.
Face-to-Face Meeting	When the person's preferred style of communication is verbal When the person does not feel threatened about giving direct feedback	Give the person enough lead time to prepare. Meet in the other person's office or in a neutral, informal setting.
Group Methods		
Anonymous, Through Small Group	When anonymous feedback is preferred When group interaction can enrich and reinforce feedback	Inform the group of the meeting's purpose and process ahead of time. Invite staff to form groups of three or four. Have each group create a list of suggestions in writing.
Open, Whole Group	When discussion and interaction are desired When candid, constructive conflict will clear the air	Inform the group of the meeting's purpose and process ahead of time. Share insights about possible problems and opportunities, and ask for reactions. Prepare to use conflict-management skills. Consider using an outside facilitator.
Diagnostic Methods		
Feedback Instruments	When there is a desire to quantify the feedback data When there is a desire to compare feedback received over time	Inform others of how you will summarize and share the data. Be sure to include open-ended questions.
Verification of Personal Assessment	When you wish to focus feedback on specific issues When discussion and interaction are desired	Distribute a written list of things you think you do well and don't do well. Ask others for agreement or disagreement, and reasons why (in writing). Inform others how you will summarize and share the data.

Guidelines for using the methods

Step 1   Set your expectations. Decide what kind of feedback you wish to get, from whom you would like to get it, and how you plan to use it.

Step 2   When you approach people, be specific in your requests. A verbal invitation is preferable to a written one. Here are three examples:

"Jose, I'm trying to learn how to be a more effective leader. I would find it valuable to get written suggestions from you regarding how effectively I handled the meetings of the design team recently. I'm sure I could have done it better. Can you put down on paper some perceptions that you think I might benefit from hearing?"

"Susan, I would like to meet with you to get some feedback on how I can improve my performance in my interactions with you and your group and how I could make better use of my time with you, especially with regard to our budget and product planning sessions. Do you have suggestions on this? Do I do anything to cause problems or create barriers? Can I meet with you next week to talk about the feedback?"

(To a group) "I'd like to improve my effectiveness as a leader, and your feedback would be really valuable. Instead of our regular meeting next week, I would like to use the time to form several groups of three or four people who would identify some specific behaviors (such as how well I am listening) or any tendencies (patience level) I have that impair our working together."

Step 3   Express sensitivity to the person's possible discomfort. Here are some examples.

"I know it may be difficult to be candid, but I want to assure you that I value both positive and negative comments. I will keep everything you say in the strictest confidence."

"What I'm asking may not be easy for you to do, but honest feedback will be very valuable both to me and to the work we do together."

Step 4   Listen carefully to the feedback. To show you understand, paraphrase accurately what you have heard.

Step 5   Thank everyone who gives you feedback.

Tips: • When you receive feedback, resist the tendency to comment or explain your behavior. If you succumb, you will stifle future feedback. You are not obligated to agree, only to accept the other person's perspective.
   • *Always* thank people for giving feedback and acknowledge the risk they took to give it to you.
   • Your choice of the six methods shown in Table 4-1 depends on the level of fear in the staff, the potential sensitivity of the feedback, and the time required to elicit the feedback.
   • Use more than one method.
   • Choose the methods that will give you the most honest and thorough feedback.
   • Make collecting personal feedback a regular part of your work together.
   • Encourage others to collect feedback as well.

Eliciting feedback on a regular basis stimulates others to follow your lead. But receiving feedback is not easy. You may not like what you hear. Specific feedback may provoke strong defensive reactions in you. How you react will have far-reaching consequences, because people will take their cue for dealing with feedback from you. Demonstrating how to accept feedback and changing your behavior as needed is where true learning will come for everyone.

For example, suppose someone informs you that you lose your temper too often. You may then wonder out loud when you have *ever* lost your temper. To deny feedback or argue the point is to deny that person's perspective. Much as you may wish to dispute the logic or the form of the feedback, resist the temptation. Effective feedback is descriptive, specific, timely, and nonjudgmental. The feedback you get may not be effectively delivered. If this happens, the skill of active listening could pay huge dividends in improving the Teach and Learn climate. Seek more information. You will improve the value of feedback by asking the person to give specific examples of when your behavior occurred, what the person felt, and how your behavior affected the person and others.

Regardless of the specifics, you must treat each person's feedback as a single case and look for validation from other sources.

You are not obligated to agree with feedback, only to accept it with a "thank you." In the long term, the most significant result of the leader's receiving feedback well comes in making it safe for others in the organization to give and receive feedback.

Helping Groups Overcome Obstacles

Leaders know the need for patience comes with the territory, and patience can be a huge challenge. Perhaps followers aren't "getting it," or they squabble endlessly with each other. Some leaders choose to roll their eyes and stay above the fray. Some choose to jump into the fray with guns blazing. Experience shows that neither the "flight" nor "fight" response is very effective in the long term.

Any number of individuals in an organization may exhibit their willingness to learn, but the groups they work in can develop "learning disabilities," or cultural habits that prevent learning, sharing knowledge, and acting upon new knowledge. Such groups may not be conscious of their learning disability, but leaders shape the cultural habits of groups and organizations.

Leaders' capacities to listen and reflect on what people have to say before they state their positions has a direct impact on the competence and confidence of the people they work with. When leaders demonstrate the perseverance and the patience to listen through the words to understand the meanings and perceptions of others, they teach others to do the same with one another.

The action orientation of many leaders makes patient behaviors extraordinarily difficult. Accustomed to making things happen, leaders fear letting go of the control they imagine they have. The fear of letting go is almost always present in leaders, who deeply feel their responsibility for achieving specific outcomes. Micromanagement is present when leaders lack trust in others' capacity to perform. It interferes with others' learning and inhibits others' interest in taking risks. Micromanagement can be quite subtle when leaders preach independent decision making, but question almost every decision they have encouraged others to make. The following example is typical of many strong leaders.

A Learning Disability Example

At first glance, Edward appears to be the antithesis of the typical micromanager. An extremely successful young entrepreneur, he is savvy, quick, and charismatic. His management team often struggles to keep up with him. A visionary, Edward has successfully reframed the future within his own industry niche. He has effectively energized his management team and developed a workforce that shares his values and goals. Because of his enormous respect for learning, he has invested heavily in training and development.

Nevertheless, planning takes a back seat to "firefighting" in the company, which operates at a furious pace. Growth and expansion are high on the list of strategic priorities. Policies and procedures are in constant states of flux. Edward knows enough about the nature of young organizations to realize that his organization must be weaned from its dependence on him, but he is so often filled with urgency that he is not able to wait for people to grow in competence and confidence. People entrusted to make decisions feel second-guessed when Edward criticizes or questions the decisions they make. Because Edward's intuition is more often right than wrong, people defer more and more decisions until they have gained Edward's input, and the organization continues to fail in creating shared power.

"He carried a ladder wherever he went. After a while, people left all the high places for him." Like the man in the epigram, Edward "carries a ladder." His personal Teach and Learn challenge is to come to grips with the fact that few people will measure up to his expectations. Despite having excellent interpersonal skills, he feels frustrated at the inability of his associates to take on their decision-making responsibilities. Single-handedly, Edward has ensured that the organization is caught in an endless loop.

Time to Move off Center Stage

At times like this, leadership behaviors become absolutely critical. Effectively supporting the decision making of others can have enormous potential leverage in generating change. It is also among the most difficult behaviors to apply, because Edward (like all leaders) is part of the system. By virtue of his position, he is the proverbial 800-pound gorilla. His words and opinions carry great weight. If others are to freely express themselves and learn, he must avoid the tendency to give his opinion at every turn in the discussion. As long as Edward maintains center stage in the debate, others will defer to his position and to his formidable intuition. Insightful teaching may occur, but others' learning will be incomplete, because once again Edward will have formulated the answers.

For genuine learning to occur, leaders like Edward, in the opinion of leadership author Ronald Heifetz, need to move away from defining problems and providing solutions. They need to move toward identifying challenges and framing key questions and issues. "Knowing" the solution tends to blind the mind to relevant facts and other possible perspectives. To learn requires leaving open the possibility of being wrong or that something unexpected or uncomfortable could happen as the result of current thinking. Learning requires trading a measure of control for a measure of ambiguity. Edward must resist the impulse to advocate his position or a favored solution and instead help others remain focused on exploring tough questions. He must ensure that people are heard and understood and that thorny, messy issues receive deep reflection over time. Edward must get off center stage and provide opportunities for the expression of many perspectives.

The leader who is intent on improving the organization's capacity to learn, must dispense with the notion of cloning herself or even duplicating her intuitive abilities in others. A lasting and durable lesson for people comes from setting the expectation that free and open inquiry is not only welcome, it is indispensable.

The following tool can help you create an environment of inquiry, to generate honest discussion, and to minimize defensiveness.

Assert and Explore: A Tool for Discovery

Purpose:
- To frame an issue clearly and honestly
- To maintain balanced participation around an issue
- To surface and process conflict

Step 1   At a meeting this week, commit to practicing the issue-framing phrases in Table 4-2 (paraphrase them if you wish). If conflict or disagreement arises, practice the set of phrases in Table 4-3.

Step 2   Distribute copies of these phrases to your colleagues. Discuss how they help to create understanding. Be receptive to the alternate responses of your colleagues.

Step 3   Set aside five minutes at the end of the meeting to discuss the effect that using these phrases had on the quality of the communication in the meeting.

Table 4-2: Advocate or Explore Ideas

Advocate	*Explore*
Use the following phrases when stating a position and explaining a train of thought:	Use the following phrases when seeking clarification or working for common understanding:
"This is what I think, and this is how I arrived at it."	"What led you to conclude that?"
"I made the assumption that..."	"Can you help me understand your thinking process in that sequence?"
"I'm not quite certain about this part—perhaps you have some suggestions."	"What do you believe is important about that?"
"The people (areas) that I think this is most likely to affect are..."	"Do you have any data that might help validate this?"
"Do you agree with my line of reasoning?"	"Let me see if I understand. You think that... Is that it?"
"Do you have anything to add to what I've considered?"	"Do you have some data I have not taken into account?"
"Do you have a different perspective?"	"I wonder if you've considered..."

Table 4-3: Raising or Processing Potential Conflict

Surface	*Process*
Use these phrases when bringing your disagreement to the surface or when presenting an alternate point of view:	Use these phrases when helping a group resolve conflict that inhibits learning:
"Did you consider...?"	"What do we know for a fact?"
"When you phrase it that way, I get concerned that it means..."	"What is it that we *don't* know?"
"I'm having difficulty with that line of reasoning because I..."	"Are we operating from different assumptions?"
"Are you basing your conclusions on data I haven't seen or understood?"	"What do you need to have to consider an alternative?"
"So if I understand you correctly, you believe that..."	"Where do we agree and where do we differ?"
	"Does anybody have ideas that might help clarify our thinking?"

Defensive Thinking

It's been said that people are not fragile, but organizations are. Organizations may learn as individuals learn, but organizational learning is much more than the sum of individual learning. This sometimes frustrating phenomenon is summed up in the often-heard lament: "How can a room full of people with an average IQ of 130 have a collective IQ of 70?"

As previously stated, learning requires both intellectual and emotional intelligence. Distrust, fear of the loss of status or power, disrespect, bias, and interpersonal differences—all conspire to diminish learning. On the other hand, trust, respect, understanding, and empathy—all foster learning. How people relate to and interact with each other in an organization profoundly affects how the organization learns.

For example, in many manufacturing organizations, a conflict develops between engineers and machinists, as engineers pit their theoretical knowledge against the practical knowledge of the machinists. Young engineers, in particular, alienate machinists by parading their theoretical knowledge. In return, machinists lose respect for the engineers because they appear not to understand how the work actually gets done or how the machine really works. Left unchecked, such differences in perspectives can escalate into conflicts that poison the atmosphere for learning.

Fundamental to understanding organizational learning is the concept of "mental models." Author Peter Senge describes mental models as "deeply held images of how the world works, images that can limit us to familiar ways of thinking and acting." Mental models are so basic to our understanding of the world that we are hardly conscious of them. Some examples of organizational mental models are as follows:

- When learning is required, training is the best solution.
- Organizations are best controlled through a management hierarchy.
- Everybody can be motivated by offering financial incentives.
- The customer is always right.
- Consensus decision making is always slow.

While these mental models (and others) are neither right nor wrong, they may not reflect current reality. Abiding by outdated and inaccurate mental models is risky and often harmful.

Two Levels of Learning

Chris Argyris, a renowned expert on organizational learning, has, for several decades, studied how organizations learn. He distinguishes between two levels of learning:

1. Learning that is characterized by simple, routine problem solving and that requires no fundamental change to our thinking or system

Example: Sales improves the quality of the reports it gives to operations concerning customer feedback on a product.
2. Breakthrough learning that directly challenges the prevailing mental model on which the system is built
Example: Sales arranges to have operations personnel interact directly with customers about the product.

On the one hand, routine problem-solving learning is an automatic response to an issue. On the other hand, breakthrough learning demands that people and groups challenge their mental models. For example, changing who should interact with the customer will challenge the mental models of sales and others. Challenging such assumptions will often meet with resistance.

Breakthrough learning must be generated, not merely applied. Because it represents a break from existing mental models, it will effectively reframe the future. Without a capacity for breakthrough learning, leaders are ill equipped to test the validity of existing mental models, which can and may have become obsolete almost overnight. Examples are everywhere. The U.S. auto industry came close to collapsing before it abandoned its outmoded mental model that quality was irrelevant to American consumers. IBM lost its dominance when it was slow to recognize the decline of mainframe computers.

Although breakthrough learning is essential to creating significant change, it may be absent among the smartest of management groups because such learning depends less on intelligence than on reflective thinking and honest dialogue. Too often, defensive reasoning and the fear of failure take over.

Paul contends with such a situation. He is the director of software engineering for Woodward Network Solutions, a medium-sized computer firm specializing in products and services for the Internet. Not surprisingly, the pace of change at Woodward is fast, and shows no signs of slowing. The company has built a reputation for solving challenging security issues. Steadily growing demand for Woodward's services has brought many bright, young software engineers into the company.

In the past two months, however, feedback from customers indicates their unhappiness with the falling quality of Woodward's services. One client is considering dropping Woodward as a supplier. When Paul brought the team together in what he hoped would be a candid exploration of the client's issues, the team members reacted defensively. Embarrassed, they blamed everything and everyone but themselves: unclear expectations, lack of adequate resources, unsupportive leadership, even an unreasonable client. Despite their acknowledged intelligence and drive to succeed, they were unable and unwilling to see how their thinking might be contributing to the client's dissatisfaction. They were stuck in their mental models, thinking that their clients were not very smart, that their leaders were out of touch, and that they knew best.

Paul could not break through their defensive reactions. These bright individuals were unable or unwilling to see things from other points of view. Learning was at a standstill.

Breakthrough learning does not often occur in difficult and threatening situations, when people get stuck in defensive thinking. Chris Argyris claimed the most common defensive behaviors are as follows:

1. Attempting to stay in control of the situation
2. Seeing things in stark black and white terms instead of shades of gray
3. Focusing on winning or losing
4. Suppressing negative feelings to protect oneself
5. Avoiding emotions, confrontation, and risk

Defensive behaviors are found in all organizations. Left unresolved, defensive thinking and the avoidance of conflict create an atmosphere that cannot sustain learning. Influence and power are not dispersed. Learning is not shared. Not knowing something is seen as a weakness, and making a mistake can be tantamount to career suicide.

The following exercise, derived from Chris Argyris's work, is designed to counteract defensive behaviors by teaching people how to reason productively, expose and confront emotional issues, and explore alternate assumptions.

Authentic Conversation: A Tool for Revealing Assumptions

Purpose:
- To break through chronic defensiveness
- To illustrate how we censor ourselves

Step 1   Select a difficult and challenging interpersonal issue that you have faced. For example:
- You believe your team is dangerously complacent
- You believe your perspective is not valued
- You are unable to reach agreement with your associates
- You believe that the organization resists change

Step 2   Write a paragraph or two describing the situation, what you are trying to accomplish, and the reactions you anticipate.

Step 3   Draw a line down the center of a sheet of paper. Recall an actual (or foresee an imaginary) conversation in which the problem is brought up. In the left-hand column, write out the dialogue as it occurred (or as you predict it will happen).

Step 4   In the right-hand column write what you were thinking and feeling, but did not openly express. Be sure to include what you were feeling.

Example:

What we said	*What I was thinking and feeling*
ME: Linda, I'd like to schedule a meeting with you next Monday to get an update on how the new project is going.	I'm really nervous that I haven't been getting any updates. I wonder if she really has a handle on this project.
LINDA: OK. But it will probably have to be late in the afternoon, because we've got a design review planned.	A design review? At this late date? They must be further behind than I thought.
ME: Fine, I understand your time crunch. Would 4:00 work out? We could meet for an hour.	Why didn't she just invite me to the design review? That could be useful, but maybe she's afraid to admit how it's really going. I won't push it.

What we said	*What I was thinking and feeling*
LINDA: I'm sure 4:00 will work out. In the conference room, then?	
ME: OK. See you there.	I'd better not offer to come to the design review. That might prove to be uncomfortable for us all.

Step 5   After a few days, come back and reflect on what you wrote:
- How did I come to think and feel this way?
- What was I trying to do?
- How did what I say contribute to the problem?
- Why didn't I say what I was thinking?
- What was I afraid would happen?
- What assumptions was I making about others in the conversation?
- What insights does this exercise bring me?
- What actions can I take to overcome defensive thinking?

Step 6   Meet with a couple of individuals who are (or could be) participants in this conversation and ask for their feedback and comments. Encourage them to complete the exercise using their own example.

Tips:
- Practice this exercise first with your peers and/or direct reports.
- Expect that your first attempts at this exercise will be awkward, like playing a violin for the first time.
- Approach the review of this exercise in a spirit of openness and inquiry.
- Be sure you frankly express feelings in the right-hand column.
- Reflect on why you made the assumptions you did.
- Ask for feedback from others about your reasoning.
- Use nonjudgmental language in your discussion of the exercise.

The greatest leverage comes in shaping how the organization learns. We have stated that the leader's task is to improve the interpersonal learning of people in the organization, starting with how the leader demonstrates his or her own learning.

Organizational Learning

Leaders have a strong role in improving organizational and technical learning. Organizational learning can be defined as the collective ability to understand the organization and its environment and to change how the parts of the organization work together. Many corporate training efforts tend to reinforce functional mindsets because they focus on helping people do their jobs better. If the aim of teaching and learning is to generate and widely disperse the power to take initiative, so the aim of corporate training must be to emphasize big-picture issues and the power to take initiative.

Larry Perlman, CEO of Ceridian, oversaw the difficult transformation of Control Data Corporation from a computer manufacturing company into a services operation. In the process, he needed to respond to the many voices of concern about where he was taking the company and why. He discovered that many in the organization lacked business competence. They were not well informed about the organization's position in the marketplace and the competitive business realities it faced. Perlman launched a large organization-wide business economics education process to help people understand the reality of what the company was up against. He said, "we literally had to teach people what a profit was—and these were smart people!"

Functional Mindsets

In "Reframe the Future," we introduced the systems map, a tool that helps people understand how their organization operates as a system and how it interacts with the outside environment. Such a tool can help employees see the big picture and give them a context within which to perform their roles in the organization.

When people do not see the big picture, they fall prey to a learning disability that Peter Senge named the "I am my position" syndrome, in which individuals pay more attention to their position within the organization than to their contribution to the purpose of the whole organization. Taking a narrow view of one's role not only blocks receptivity to new learning, but it also tends to slow the transfer of learning to the organization as a whole.

This functional mindset (sometimes referred to as "operating within organizational silos") prevents people in the organization from working effectively together because it tends to promote functional goals over system-wide goals. For example, Sales maximizes its sales goals and creates a demand for products or services that operations cannot produce. Purchasing saves money on materials and passes greater costs on to manufacturing. Such short-sighted thinking occurs with regularity in many organizations.

One of the most common outcomes of the "I am my position" phenomenon is the promotion of competition for scarce resources between functions. When the mission and direction of the company are not clear, the functions tend to fend for themselves, and people turn their focus from the outside customer to their own areas of concern. This mindset is discussed further in Chapter 6, "Balance Paradox."

Typically, management teams are no more receptive to learning than are other parts of the organization. The interpersonal dynamics and the power needs of executives tend to make collective inquiry seem threatening. The following exercise is a tool to broaden the perspective of executives and help them work more closely together.

In Another Person's Shoes: A Tool for System Perspective

Purpose:
- Provide an experiential perspective of how the organization operates as a system
- Improve professional trust and communication between managers

Step 1   Meet with the management team and outline the following plan: In the next year, each executive will be expected to "swap" roles with another executive for a period of four weeks, forming a Learning Partnership.

- Learning Partners:
    Determine when they would like to trade roles
    Prepare each other and others for the new role
    Stay in regular contact with each other throughout the swap
    Relocate to each other's office during the period of the swap
    Make all decisions as necessary and do not defer decisions past the four-week period
    Confer with each other at any time
- Subordinates and other associates will view their interim manager as a fully empowered substitute for their permanent manager and are expected to actively support and teach their interim manager during the swap.
- Personnel decisions, such as performance reviews, will be conducted jointly by the Learning Partners.

Step 2   Each Learning Partnership meets with the senior executive before their swap occurs:
- To provide a plan and dates for the swap
- To determine learning objectives for each person
- To set ground rules regarding confidentiality and performance issues
- To raise and discuss potentially sensitive issues that may be encountered

Step 3   Learning partners do the swap.

Step 4   Each Learning Partnership meets with the senior leader after the swap:
- To review lessons learned
- To exchange insights and constructive feedback about each area

Step 5   As soon as possible or at year end, assemble all Learning Partnerships together to capture and summarize lessons learned.

Tips: • This exercise works well at the senior level of the organization. It does not work well when jobs are highly technical and require specialized knowledge.
      • Do not attempt this exercise if the interpersonal trust level is low among the members of the management team.
      • The four-week period enables the learners to absorb the role fully and engage in the work required. A shorter period is possible, but it will yield less value.
      • Key communication links should be established. Customer relationships should be addressed.
      • Because of the special circumstances, performance in the alternate role should not be evaluated on any criterion other than that the person put forth a good faith effort to learn.

Connecting with Customers

One of the most powerful means of helping people improve their competence in understanding how the organization works is to connect them with customers. Every organization, public or private, has customers—the constituency to which the organization owes its very existence. When employees hear and respond to customers, they are literally connected to the lifeblood of the organization. Their enhanced perspective about the work of the organization broadens dramatically. They are in a much better position to understand how their work contributes to the organizational mission and how they may have to adapt to the work of competitors who also want to serve their customers.

We recall a steel manufacturer that created specialty products for demanding customers. A salesperson spent several weeks attempting to understand how to do a simple redesign of a part that would meet a customer's needs. In conversation, the sales manager suggested that the worker who would make the part pay a visit to the customer's site. The visit lasted all of 15 minutes; in that time the worker quickly grasped what was needed.

In service organizations, most contact with customers is through front-line workers. In product organizations, the same front-line workers may never see the customer or know how the customer uses their product. Meaningful customer interaction happens only through sales, marketing, or senior managers. Such organizations miss opportunities not only for employees to learn, but also for employees to contribute added value.

The following exercise is designed to push learning deep into the organization through interactions between employees and the customers that the organization serves.

Face-to-Face: A Tool for Connecting with Customers

Purpose:
- Put employees in real-time contact with their customers.
- Create a database of information about specific current and future customer needs.
- Generate the momentum for process improvement.

Step 1   Define the customer base:
- Identify customers by company.
- Identify key contacts at each company.

Step 2   Bring together a cross-section of employees and managers to:
- Design a customer interview guide (see page 112).
- Select two-person employee teams to interview customers.
- Match each employee team with a customer.

Step 3   Provide training on the use of the customer interview guide:
- Discuss purpose, protocol, and expected outputs of interview.
- Discuss the interview questions.
- Practice role-playing the interview.

Step 4   Schedule and conduct face-to-face customer interviews:
- Record the data.

- Record other comments and questions.

Step 5   Follow up on customer interviews:
- Address any immediate customer needs identified.
- Thank customers.
- Relate back to peers in small structured sessions the outcomes of the interviews.
- Summarize the data at the corporate level.

Step 6   Conduct a session of all customer interview teams with management:
- Publish summarized reports of interview data corporate-wide.
- Follow up with customers where appropriate.
- Incorporate what was learned into strategic planning.

Customer interview guide should include variations on these questions:
- What do you like about our products and/or services?
- What do you need from us?
- How do you use what we provide you?
- Are there any gaps between what you need and what you get?
- How will we know when your needs have been successfully met?
- What can we improve upon?

Tips:
- Be careful not to set up employee teams for failure (for example, interviewing an obviously angry customer).
- Match employees with customers they have some familiarity with or interest in.
- Select employee teams so at least one person has strong interviewing skills.
- Provide employee teams with guidance on what they can commit to and what they can't.
- Although managers may be included in employee teams, focus on getting front-line employees in front of customers.
- Respect the data that employees gather from the customer.

- Expect some anxiety on the part of employee teams; take time to practice "what if" situations.
- *Always* follow through on any commitments made to customers.

Technical Learning

As employees more clearly understand how the organizational system collaborates to provide value to customers, they discover the need to improve their technical learning, their ability to fulfill their roles within the organization. Every time the future is reframed, shock waves of change invariably roll out to every corner of the organization as jobs are redefined, new technology is introduced, and internal relationships are redrawn. Are people prepared and enabled to address such changes?

Learning: Reflection vs. Action

Organizations tend to approach learning and change from one of two extremes, either with a bias for reflection—an orientation to planning and preparing—or with a bias for action—an orientation to do things quickly. Organizations that approach learning from a reflective perspective may decide on the conceptual level what needs to happen, but fail to act decisively on that decision. Stuck in a reflective mindset, they spend hours planning, making endless revisions, and expanding the time frames for change. Similarly, an organization may overuse formal training as the primary means for initiating change. The change effort bogs down as the organization keeps "backing up for a good start."

On the other hand, acting without sufficient reflection has its own risks. Organizations that are prone to perpetual action tend to become "fixated on firefighting," which is another learning disability described by Senge. Of course, some firefighting is a fact of life in any organization, but it becomes cancerous when the firefighters fail to see long-term patterns and condemn themselves to reacting.

People in the organization become so practiced in fixing today's problems that they become quite adept at resolving them. In a worst-case scenario, the rewards and attention they get may induce people to cause problems so that they can resolve them and save the day! The typical result of the "fixation on firefighting" is that new problems tend to arise from the solutions applied to previous problems. Constant firefighting precludes breakthrough learning, because the fixes are focused strictly on today with little thought given to tomorrow.

Neither extreme generates true learning. Reflection without action fails because insights remained untested. Action without reflection fails because it is little more than "reaction," and insight is not generated at all. Both are necessary. On the interplay of reflection and action, author-consultant Richard Pascale has suggested that we are more likely to "act our way into a new way of thinking than think our way into a new way of acting." This may especially be true for organizations, because taking action (based on insights from reflection) can promote a spirit of experimentation, generate momentum, and demonstrate visible progress. Organizations are most likely to challenge their outdated mental models when they are forced to act from different ones.

Spreading Learning

If knowledge is viewed as power, people tend to think of it as something to accumulate and hoard so that they can enhance their own worth in the organization. Organizations become crippled when this behavior becomes widespread.

Sam is a brilliant technician in a small manufacturing company. He has no peer in the organization when it comes to using a multispindle industrial lathe to fashion a stainless steel part with tolerances 100 times smaller than the diameter of a human hair. But for whatever reason, Sam either can't or won't share what he knows with other technicians so that the entire company might benefit. Organizations cannot afford such loner behaviors. Sooner or later, Sam's job will be in jeopardy. Sam is also cutting himself off from learning from others. He will not get even better because his knowledge will ultimately be outdated. Organizations are populated by specialists armed with vast knowledge and little ability to communicate it. Increasingly, such specialists are less valuable than other (perhaps less knowledgeable) people who multiply their value by sharing what they know with others. Why is this? Because knowledge becomes more valuable to all parties when it is shared. Knowledge that is shared can be magnified faster, acted upon by more people, and adopted more widely than knowledge that is hoarded. In addressing the challenge of teaching and learning, leaders must amend the saying "knowledge is power" to "*shared* knowledge is power."

Summary

The principal output of Teach and Learn is to generate knowledge and to disperse the power to act throughout the whole organization. Shared learning is the basis for unleashing new energy.

Learning is the individual and collective ability of people to reflect on past behavior, identify alternatives, and change how they act. The role of the leader is to improve the organization's competence and confidence to learn.

The greatest influence leaders have on improving the capacity of the organization to teach and learn is through personal example. When leaders demonstrate their willingness and capacity to learn, they profoundly shape how the organization deals with learning. Interpersonal learning is helped immeasurably by collecting feedback.

Through mindful use of language, leaders can create an environment more receptive to learning. The leader's principal role is to remove obstacles, recognize and confront learning disabilities, and ultimately "get off center stage" so that others can contribute.

For organizational learning to occur, people must confront their functional mindsets. Sharing with others what external customers and stakeholders need helps provide a big-picture perspective.

Effective learning balances reflection and action. Thoughtful action creates momentum and stimulates feedback and additional learning. The power to act cannot be generated and distributed throughout the organization unless learning and knowledge are freely shared.

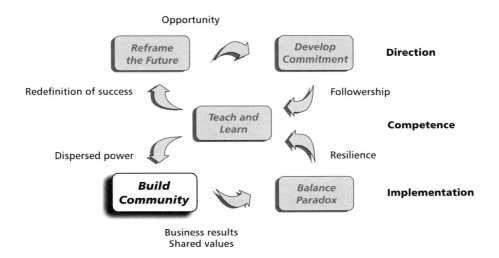

Opportunity

Reframe the Future

Develop Commitment

Direction

Redefinition of success

Followership

Teach and Learn

Competence

Dispersed power

Resilience

Build Community

Balance Paradox

Implementation

Business results
Shared values

CHAPTER 5

Build Community

> If I am only for myself, what am I?
> If I am not for myself, who am I?
>
> *—Hillel*

Richard, the president of a small pharmaceutical company, decided it was time for significant change. The organization had begun to lose its competitive advantage in the marketplace. On the advice of a trusted colleague, he hired a consultant to take the management group through a strategic planning process. Because Richard was pleased with the process and the results, he eagerly shared the group's newly crafted strategy and plan with the employees. Not surprisingly their initial response signaled their wholehearted support. Six months later, Richard questioned his leadership capabilities. Little had changed; business went on largely as it always had. And Richard relearned that defining direction, communicating intent, and gaining employee buy-in are insufficient to bring about a required change. He felt as though he were captain of a ship that had no rudder. He had the responsibility of establishing direction, but felt powerless to influence the course of events. Today, he knows that the members of the board of directors are concerned and that his job and the success of his organization are on the line.

In desperation, Richard has hired another organizational consultant, whose assessment has indicated that employees understand and agree with the proposed direction, are content in their jobs, and believe that Richard is a capable leader. This consultant claims that the organization lacks sufficient leadership talent to move the change process forward. Although the managers may want the organization to be different, the employees are comfortably working as they always have.

From the second consultant, Richard has also learned that he has been a hub-and-spoke leader. Significantly, his direct reports habitually come to his office to ask him for a little advice and a lot of permission. Seldom has he encouraged them to think and act on their own. Nor has he encouraged people to work together. He prizes being the master arbiter in all disputes. Given the enormous business challenges that lie before the organization, Richard realizes that he needs people who can think deeply about strategic and tactical issues, can partner with each other to bridge functions, and can be honest sounding boards for one another. Richard must face the fact that he has been the primary constraint to organizational growth. He must change his leadership style.

Previously, having employees execute defined tasks was one of the major sources of strength in his organization. Now, having people take calculated risks, make suggestions, and work together must be an organizational strength. Richard must build an organization that will look and operate unlike any he is familiar with. He and his direct reports have not been appropriate role models. Today, most of his energy goes into thinking about what the organization should look like, feel like, and act like, and how to effect the change.

According to the consultant, the employees are frustrated by their inability to make the necessary transitions to new ways to work together. They are simultaneously torn between fear of not having the requisite skills and excitement about the possibilities outlined in the strategic plan. Without the support of strong leaders and the tools to move forward, people will remain bound by their fears. At the very moment when all the parties should come together to address their concerns, each remains isolated and silent, in the hope that the threat of change will evaporate.

Workplace Community

At the start of the Industrial Revolution hierarchical organizations were designed to manage an uneducated workforce within a relatively stable environment. Hierarchies were fairly rigid structures, in which roles and responsibilities were clearly defined. The unintended responsibility of the employee within such an organization was to make the boss look good.

In today's economy, many leaders know that the source of competitive advantage lies in a workforce that is flexible, nimble, adaptable, and able to integrate diverse functions. Given a change in strategy, a new organizational structure is required. In the new organization, it is important that all employees focus on satisfying the needs of the customer. They must move from limited areas of responsibility and accountability to being responsible for planning, coordinating, creating, contributing, and doing, which encompasses a significant, yet critical organizational challenge. Expectations for leaders and employees alike clearly have risen. All employees are asked to work together more intensely. The constraint to organizational success is not money; it is employee time and talent—not the skills of individuals, but the sum total of the ability of all individuals in teams and cross-functional groups to work together effectively.

As Richard and his managers found, most employees expect more from the organization than a place to put in time and take out a paycheck. They expect to participate in planning what and how work will be performed; they want to find meaning at work; they want to know that their work makes a difference. The requirement of businesses to operate in competitive environments and the desire of employees to find meaning at work increasingly converge.

In the recent past, people with similar interests, often within defined geographic boundaries, formed communities. They experienced community in their neighborhoods or through their religious affiliations. Today, 75 percent of Americans don't know their neighbors. Such indicators of societal dissatisfaction as levels of violence, divorce, and self-destructive behavior have increased. Although we have the technical capabilities to improve communication significantly, people often feel disassociated from the larger society. The human need to belong to a larger whole remains as more people experience fewer places to find it. Leaders who recognize this vacuum understand the attraction that a well-designed business organization can have for their employees.

In response to changing human demands, new workplace structures are emerging and significantly altering the expectations of leaders and employees. At their core, the new structures are designed to encourage collaboration across functional specialties, to encourage partnering between business entities, and to connect employees more closely with customers and suppliers. Moving in these three directions allows more efficient use of resources, sustains innovation, and enables higher levels of customer satisfaction.

New workplace structures redefine what is discussed, how it is discussed, what is measured, what is considered risky, who makes decisions, and how rewards are distributed. In these new structures, employees:

- Participate in common practices
- Depend on one another
- Identify themselves as a part of something larger than the sum of their individual relationships
- Commit themselves for the long term to their own, one another's, and the organization's well being

(Shaffer and Anundsen, 1993)

Well-managed organizations feel like communities to the people who work in them and care about them. The major leadership challenges in creating new workplace structures include:

- Integrating individuals with diverse skills, interests, and values
- Integrating diverse geographical locations, etc.
- Increasing the collective intelligence of the enterprise
- Creating an extraordinary level of trust
- Developing creativity in resolving and anticipating problems
- Creating flexible organizational boundaries

(Gozdz, 1995)

Leaders must do all of the above while they build a work environment in which everyone accomplishes their personal ambitions while they contribute to a meaningful whole.

Elements of Workplace Community

The elements listed below are critical to workplace community:

- Leadership
- Core strategy
- Structure consistent with strategy
- Work processes that make sense
- Defined roles
- Workforce competence
- Measures of performance

The remainder of this chapter expands on these elements and provides the tools to accomplish them.

Leadership

Historically the leader was held responsible for the success of the organization. Although someone must ultimately be in charge, having a single leader in an organization is insufficient. At a particular stage in the life cycle of the organization or during a specific crisis or opportunity, a single leader will not have all the strengths required. Leadership is a function not a person. A group of people working together as a leadership team can bring many strengths to an organization. Together they can address the five challenges presented in this book.

Each member of the leadership team is usually charged with maximizing the effectiveness of the particular operation over which he or she is directly responsible. The result can be a considerable amount of internal competitiveness. Overcoming internal competition requires establishing the role of the leadership group in determining new products and services, a respectful work environment, the allocation of resources, and the development and implementation of organizational strategy. A portion of each member's compensation should be at risk, based on their delivery. The leadership team must:

- Be concerned with the quality of their interaction and be ready to move the organization forward. Building community requires leaders to operate and function as a team
- Bring conflict to the surface and deal with it
- Demonstrate an extraordinary level of people skills
- Learn continuously
- Understand the fundamentals of total quality principles
- Use creative approaches to problem solving
- Perceive the organization as a whole system
- Demonstrate sufficient emotional strength to work through adversity

Exercise: Assess Leadership Strength

Purpose: This exercise should be completed before major organizational transformation or change. It will provide a general overview of the leadership talent in the organization.

Step 1   Draw a picture of your organization. Do not draw an organization chart, which will limit rather than enhance the work that follows.

Step 2   Make a list of the people you rely on to complete major projects or to implement change, or from whom you seek council.

Estimate the strengths and weaknesses of each person according to the above dimensions. Locate the individuals on the picture you completed in Step 1.

Step 3   Answer the following questions:
- Do you rely on a relatively few people?
- Does the organization have sufficient leadership strength to move forward? If not, where are the strengths and weaknesses?
- Are those who have the leadership strengths in leadership positions?
- Do the people with leadership capabilities understand and share your vision for the business? Are they willing to do what is necessary to make it happen? Can you rely on them?
- Do leaders work together effectively?

Step 4   If leadership capacities fall short of organizational requirements:
- How will you develop the necessary talent?
- What will you do to promote or inhibit leadership development in your organization?
- What will you do to encourage leaders and potential leaders to overcome their local concerns and focus on the well-being of the total organization?

Step 5   Develop a one-page strategy to develop leaders in your organization. Include the following:
- Changes in your leadership style
- Changes in recruiting and staffing practices
- Leadership development activities

Step 6   Share your strategy with someone who can help, perhaps a Human Resources professional. You will want to share with that person your assessment of the leadership capabilities of the people on your list and jointly develop an improvement plan.

Core Strategy

Leaders encourage people to work together for the welfare of the whole. People must have a shared understanding of the purpose of the organization, how they will interact with each other, and how they can support the strategic intent. Core strategy is composed of four components: vision, mission, objectives, and values. Creating a single, shared definition of each term across the organization is a leadership act.

Vision

Vision defines what the organization wishes to become. A good vision statement is:

1. Memorable: Less than 25 words in length and interesting
2. Educational: Tells the audience what you are intending to accomplish
3. Inspirational: Creates enthusiasm for action and pride
4. Measurable: Defines when the vision will be achieved

Ineffective vision statements typically are wrought by a committee. They follow the formula: "We are the leader in XYZ industry, and we strive for ultimate customer satisfaction." Such a commonplace vision is unlikely to call people to action. It will be hung on walls throughout the company and seldom used to guide decision making. The following are several suggestions for developing an effective vision.

Exercise: Complete a Future State Analysis

An example of a future state analysis appears in Table 5-1.

Step 1   Create a task force of five to eight people from across the organization.

Step 2   Describe in general terms what to accomplish over the next 5–10 years.

Step 3   Determine 6–10 critical dimensions that are central to the strategy.

Table 5-1: Example of Future State Analysis

Dimension	Current State	Future State
Customers	Small companies, all are located in the U.S.	Large companies, most located within the U.S., but some are in Europe
Products/services	Focus is on products	Focus is on service
Sales process	Sales force	Sales force augmented by distributors
Employees	Primarily focused on departmental objectives	Balance of focus between the needs of customers and the organization
	Work independently	Work on cross-functional teams
Organizational competencies	Great technical skills	Project management skills
		Customer relationship skills
		Team skills

Step 4   Develop current and future states for each of the dimensions.

Step 5   (Optional) Create another column labeled "potential objectives." In this column list the objectives needed to reach the desired future state.

Step 6   Publish the result as a basis for discussion with employees.

Step 7   Gather employee input and feedback, and alter the analysis as appropriate.

Use of Imagery

The most effective vision statements incorporate imagery:

- Twenty-four ounces of Coke at arms reach anywhere in the world by the year 2010 (Coca-Cola)

- Toward Man's full life (Medtronic)
- Man on the moon by the end of the decade (John Kennedy)
- Encircle Caterpillar (Komatsu)
- Global network news (CNN)
- Put a computer on every desk (Microsoft)
- Six Hondas in a two-car garage (Honda)

The language of imagery is fresh and exciting. Vision statements are designed to energize performance. They encourage people to overcome their differences and unite to serve a larger purpose. But putting a select few people around a table for a planning session will generally not spawn compelling imagery. Rather, we recommend involving many stakeholders in the exercise.

Exercise: Develop Imagery for the Vision

Purpose: Create a compelling vision for the organization

Step 1   Develop a presentation of what the organization desires to become, based on the future state analysis created above.

Step 2   Develop a set of questions to stimulate thought about that future state. For example:
- What will our customers experience when we have achieved our vision?
- How will our products/services change the world?
- Who will benefit? In what ways?
- How will we be different as a result of the new vision?
- What could we accomplish that would be so great that it scares us to think about it?
- What benefit will our product deliver to future generations?
- What legacy does this new vision allow us to leave behind?

Step 3   Ask a small group of stakeholders to:
- Develop a slogan that captures the vision
- Draw a picture that captures the vision

Try this process with a number of groups over several months

Step 4 Ask a larger group of stakeholders to come together to view the results of the work accomplished by individuals and small groups. You will know you have established your vision when:

• The natural enthusiasm of people surfaces
• The vision is seen as invigorating and as a source of optimism
• The vision is consistent with the future state analysis

Step 5 Don't publish the result just yet. Treat the vision as tentative until you are comfortable that it:

• Energizes people
• Helps define what will and will not be undertaken
• Helps people work together

When building the vision, create objectives that the organization can digest. Sometimes it is helpful to establish a vision that has stepping stones. This creates an understanding that the vision will happen in stages. An example of the stepping-stone approach appears in Figure 5-1.

If the future cannot be imagined, it cannot be created.

Use of the Mission Statement

Mission statements define purpose, or why the organization exists. They delimit what will and will not be accomplished. For example:

• We make X product for the Y market.
• We make light bulbs.
• We provide air transportation for people and freight.

Mission statements provide an opportunity to reexamine the business's central purpose. Over time, changes may be required because of changing customer requirements, new technology, the availability of substitutes, or new competitor strategies. The output of reframing the future in Chapter 2 could have a significant

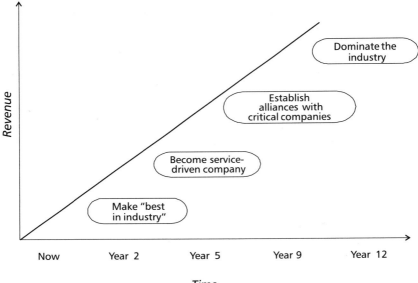

Figure 5-1: Example of Stepping Stone Approach in a Vision Exercise

impact on the mission of the organization. The next exercise identifies whether an existing business purpose should be altered.

Exercise: Develop a Mission Statement

Purpose: To develop a mission statement

Step 1   Develop questions designed to stimulate new thinking about the organization. (You may refer to similar exercises from Chapter 2.) For example:
- If our customers did not have our products or services what would they do?
- If our customers could repackage our products and services, what would they look like?
- What will our customers expect of our products and services five years from now?

- What could make our products and services obsolete?
- Given our current organizational skill set, what could we produce/deliver that would be more interesting or profitable?

Step 2   Assemble a cross-functional group with an informed perspective of the customer, market, industry, and so on. Instruct them to be truthful, and direct. Ask them to address the above questions.

Step 3   Take the information, reflect on the business's purpose, and develop a simple sentence that describes the current business purpose.

Example

Jewelry, Inc. was a family-owned business for more than 50 years. Its traditional customers were regional jewelry chains in the Midwest. Competition recently became significantly greater, and margins deteriorated. Seven years ago the management team recognized the potential for serving large national chains such as Sears, Penney's, and Wal-Mart. The answers to the above questions indicated that its new customers could benefit from the marketing and sales know-how of the company. Jewelry buyers in large retail companies, who were often saddled with a variety of responsibilities, were unlikely to have a deep knowledge of the industry. As a result, they purchased on price. Although many companies could manufacture low-cost jewelry, few had Jewelry Inc.'s information systems and marketing and sales skills. The company changed its mission from "we manufacture, market, and sell low-cost jewelry to regional and national department stores" to " we offer jewelry and marketing programs." Jewelry, Inc. further defined specific components of its marketing programs to include customized assortments, information management, and displays. Providing marketing services meant that the company was free to shift its manufacturing efforts to products where it had a competitive advantage. It was free to partner with other jewelry manufacturing companies. Thus it moved from being a jewelry manufacturer to being a jewelry sales and marketing organization.

The Use of Values

Values, the third component of the core strategy, describe the behaviors and operating principles required to achieve the vision. Values stretch employees and encourage self-examination. When a shift of vision and mission takes place, the list of values should be reviewed to ensure that they remain consistent with the direction of the business. For example, an organization that thrived for the last 30 years because of its quality technical services was forced to reexamine its values. The management group decided the organization should become much closer to the customer. Making a profit, operating as if each employee owned the business, and maintaining absolute integrity had served the organization well in the past. Internal teamwork, concern for the problems of the customer, and an emphasis on continual learning would serve the organization in the future. Jewelry, Inc.'s leadership team also revised the values statement and began the hard work of upholding the new values.

When they are modeled by senior management and used to influence everyday behavior, values can significantly shape the interactions between individuals within the organization. For example, one company president believes in the power of the contracts that individuals make with each other. Fulfilling mutually established expectations develops trust between people. She refers to the contract as "the promise." Employees and customers alike are expected to fulfill their mutually established expectations. Whenever customers fail to meet the terms of the contract, employees have the authority to cancel relationships with that client. In the early days of Digitex Corporation CEO Harry Peterson wondered if the company was going to survive. Survival was a daily concern. Yet, when a vice president succeeded in meeting financial sales targets, but failed to meet the mutually established diversity objective, Peterson reduced his bonus. Thus, Peterson signaled that was not only important that the organization survived, but how it survived.

Many leaders underestimate employee interest and concern for the values of the organization. Employees want to know the boundaries around their internal and external work relationships.

Table 5-2: Values and the Behaviors Associated with Living Them

Value	*Examples of Behaviors*
Focus on the customer	Seek customer feedback
	Understand how products and services are used by customers so we can add value
	Take customer complaints seriously
Create a learning environment	Give employees the tools and skills to process information
	Share best practices through group processes
	Encourage employees to take on new assignments
	Develop a learning plan for each employee
Demonstrate leadership in our marketplace	Join appropriate professional associations and actively participate in their activities
	Work to ensure that products and services are ranked best in class

Customers want to do business with ethical and fair suppliers. Employees want to understand the rules. Leaders increase commitment whenever they define values, live them, and ensure that they are integral to the way the organization does business. One cannot build community without values. Table 5-2 shows examples of values and the behaviors associated with living them.

Exercise: Create the Organization's Values

Purpose: To create organizational values

Step 1   Review the vision and the mission of the organization.

List the key stakeholders in the organization: customers, suppliers, owners, and employees.

Step 2   Ask representatives from each stakeholder group to define what is important to them in relating with your organization.

Given the strategic direction of the organization, ask how the various stakeholders will need to operate/interact differently.

Step 3   List the values that will guide the organization and its critical stakeholders to success.

Select the five values that are critical.

Step 4   Define each of the selected values.

Step 5   Determine the values that the leadership group wants to deepen within the organization.

Communicate the values, their importance, and the benefits associated with living them.

Step 6   Ask the members of the leadership group what they will do to live these values and how they will hold each other accountable.

Step 7   Once the group has demonstrated that they can live the values, and they have changed their behaviors, they can develop approaches to ensure that the values are lived in the rest of the organization.

Objectives

Objectives, the fourth element of core strategy, are not the nice "to do's," but the "have to do's." Objectives are the few things that must be accomplished for the organization to achieve its vision. Limiting the number of objectives helps to ensure that they will be achieved. For example:

- At least 50 percent of new customers are derived from our targeted markets.
- At least 60 percent of our clients rate our service as greatly exceeding their expectations.
- Our dealer network system is capable of selling our product worldwide.
- Manufacturing expenses this year are 15 percent less than last year.

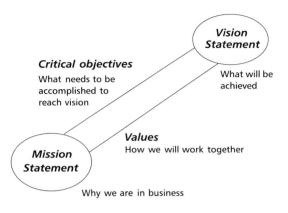

Figure 5-2: Graphic Representation of Core Strategy

Communicating Core Strategy

Leaders feel a sense of completion when they have developed and communicated the strategy; they do not realize the major effort required to achieve the change that lies before them.

It is helpful to lay out the core strategy on a single page. The example above shows the integration of the mission, vision, values, and objectives. Such a graphic representation can be a powerful tool in helping employees understand the strategy and their potential role in bringing it to fruition. We can't emphasize enough the value of creating a graphic representation of the strategy. Figure 5-2 includes the four elements above, and facilitates communication.

Deepening Core Strategy: Stories

Chapters 2 and 3 described approaches to developing stories. A powerful way to communicate core strategy is to create a story around its origin and implementation. Stories provide a powerful vehicle for helping employees further understand the mission that the organization wishes to achieve, why the values are important, and the way it intends to do so through the critical objectives.

Large-Scale Change

New group facilitation methods have been developed to accommodate 50–100 or more people simultaneously working to finalize core strategy. Two such methods are Future Search, developed by Marvin Weisbord, and Real Time Strategic Change, developed by Kathleen Dannemiller. Through group meetings, employees come to understand the core strategy and become committed to its achievement. Employees from all levels of the organization are invited to attend one- to three-day sessions. Participants are assigned seating to ensure that the whole organization is represented at each table. During the sessions they:

- Develop insight about what is happening in the environment
- Develop insight how customers and other key stakeholders view the organization
- Review the core strategy and recommend changes
- Determine specific action steps required to achieve the strategy
- Set major objectives
- Commit to work on specific projects

Because the needs and expectations of each organization are different, no standard format can be applied, and significant planning time will be needed. A qualified consultant can be very helpful. The investment of time and effort in this session will yield considerable benefits to the organization. The experiences of companies, large and small, suggest that by using large group meetings, time to implement plans is shortened and employee morale is improved.

Structure

A significant shift in the core strategy requires people to work together in different ways. Often changes in core strategy result in a change in the structure of the organization. Most leaders assume that this means restructuring the whole organization. But shifting accountabilities will be unlikely to have an insignificant impact on the company. Leaders who see restructuring as their primary means to effect change will find themselves frequently repeating the exercise.

In a major insight during a strategic planning session, Mary realized that her engineering consulting firm had great testing facilities and excellent engineers. To achieve the vision, the engineers needed to develop a broad understanding of the needs of customers and integrate the services they provided. The current organizational structure encouraged people to focus on the performance of their unit only. Mary's first attempts at reconfiguring the organization chart failed to materially affect business results. Eventually, she realized that she needed to lower the walls between functions by creating teams of people who would focus on the needs of specific customers. Further, to be effective, each of the teams would require leaders.

To ensure continued engineering excellence, the organization maintained the traditional functional hierarchy. In addition, cross-functional teams were given responsibility for developing greater understanding of the requirements of their customers and coordinating their work. The leadership team was composed of those individuals responsible for traditional areas of the business and those individuals with leadership accountability for service to customers. The new organization appears in Table 5-3.

After several years of experience with the above organizational configuration, it became clear that the company had developed significant expertise within specific industries. For example, the Exxon team had learned how to work together and deliver supe-

Table 5-3: New Organizational Structure

Customer/Leader	Environmental Engineering	Construction Engineering	Laboratory
Xerox/John	Frank	Mary	Susan
Wal-Mart/George	Gretchen	John	David
Exxon/Harry	Harry	Mary	Peter

Table 5-4: The Expanded Refinery Group

Refinery Team Leader	Environ- mental Engineering	Construction Engineering	Laboratory	Marketing	Sales
Harry	Harry	Mary	Peter	Mark	Pat

rior service to an oil company. It had developed new processes and new products that attracted other customers in the oil industry. The group expanded its role and actively marketed its services to other refineries. The expanded refinery group appears in Table 5-4.

Ability to Work in Teams

The above example illustrates how teams can become the means for accomplishing significantly higher levels of productivity. Yet anyone who has been responsible for making teams effective knows how challenging the task can be. Teams pose an increasing need for collaboration among professionals in different specialties.

The model in Figure 5-3 suggests two critical aspects of developing and operating an effective team. The first phase focuses on getting ready to work together and understanding team process. This phase is known as building the productive capability of the team. The second phase focuses on production, or doing the work for which the team was formed. Most leaders of teams move too quickly into the production phase. Their teams lack a proper foundation.

Figure 5-3 and Table 5-5 could be used to help team members focus less on resolving personality issues and more on team process and production.

Exercise: Improving the Team's Productive Capability

Step 1 Develop questions for each of the five team processes. For example:
- Plan

  Is our core strategy—vision, mission, values, and objectives—clear?

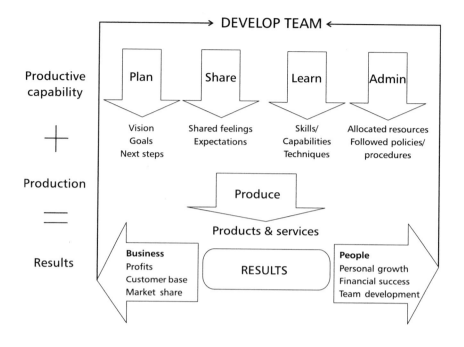

Figure 5-3: A Model for Team Productivity

> Do we have an action plan for the next six months to one year?
>
> Does each individual know what he or she is accountable for achieving?
>
> Does each individual have a personal development plan?
>
> Are weekly production schedules in place?

- Share

> Have we set aside time to discuss our feelings and concerns?
>
> Do we openly discuss our expectations?
>
> Are we setting up an environment that allows learning?
>
> Do we have ground rules in place that govern how we work together?

Table 5-5: Purposes and Examples of the Five Team Processes

Type	Purpose	Examples
Phase 1. Productive Capability		
Plan	• Develop a future scenario based on the new set of realities. • Create a desire to achieve a different outcome by establishing a goal and determining what must be done to reach it. • Investigate changes in the voice of the customer, marketplace, or critical competencies.	• Team one-year plan • Individual's life plan • Plan to install new process • Schematic of new factory • Marketing plan
Share	• Create common bonds and greater understanding by relating personal experiences and perspectives. • Share concerns and clarify expectations.	• Personal experiences of past • Frustrations with another person • Concern about a course of action
Learn	• Acquire new capabilities to improve performance or personal satisfaction. • Establish realistic expectations. • Determine faster more effective ways of achieving the goal.	• New job skills • Interpersonal skills • Business skills
Administer	• Perform those maintenance functions required to sustain the team.	• Complete budget • Fill an open position • Communicate news from home office
Phase 2. Production		
Produce	• Build products/deliver services	• Make widgets • Job training • Deliver pizza

- Learn

   Do we review our performance and learn from our successes and mistakes?

   Are individuals developing new skills and talents so we can operate more effectively?

   What competencies do we need to develop so that we can produce better products and services in the future?

   Are we taking risks?

- Administer

   Are we managing our financial resources effectively?

   Are we hiring the right kinds of people?

   Do we deal effectively with poorly performing team members?

   Have we established meetings and other forms of communication so that we operate with the greatest amount of information?

- Produce

   Are we achieving the production/service targets we have established?

   If not, which of our production processes are deficient?

Step 2	To distribute the leadership functions within the team, establish process champions—people who ensure that each of the five team processes are visible for the team. For example, a person who has strategic skills and vision could be asked to lead the planning process. An individual with good financial skills or knowledge of procedures could be asked to lead the administrative function of the team.
Step 3	Define the roles and expectations for the leader of each process. Specify the expected outcomes for each process.
Step 4	Set aside time during team meetings to focus team processes.
Step 5	Every few months review the questions in Step 1 to identify where to spend your team meeting time.

Process Leaders

As organizations become more customer, market, or quality focused, it becomes obvious that the traditional, functionally oriented structure is insufficient. It becomes imperative that the company create ways for people to work across functional lines. For example, review the engineering consulting firm example. Midlevel process managers can be expected to perform horizontal leadership across functions. They ensure that the right people are working together as a team, that cross-functional objectives are being achieved and timetables met, and that the whole team learns how to improve future performance. Process leaders should have high visibility in the organization. Because they typically are given less authority than functional leaders, they must have greater interpersonal skills. The responsible leader's job is to ensure that there is an appropriate balance between functional and process leaders.

Process at the Enterprise Level

Frank was the founder and president of MicroTech, a 10-year-old microchip test equipment manufacturer. The traditional indicators of company performance led most of his managers to believe that the company was tremendously successful. But Frank was concerned. He saw a high level of stress among employees and was acutely aware of reaching human limits. Frank hired a consultant to analyze the business.

While developing the simple map shown in Figure 5-4, Frank came to understand how real his concerns about the future potential of the organization were.

- He had always pictured the organization in terms of functions and their specific accountabilities. Developing a process map helped him see how the functions had to be deeply and integrally involved with several processes. For example, the engineering group was involved with every major process. Frank saw the need to structure the organizational goals and his leadership style to encourage cross-functional participation.

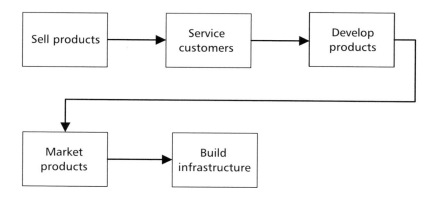

Figure 5-4: MicroTech Current Process Map

He also saw a need to hire or to develop engineers who understood the business and could relate to professional staff in all the other functions.

- Frank realized that under his direction salespeople had chased orders merely to make their revenue targets. Many large, new orders did not meet the criteria for the long-term direction needed by the company. Engineers and customer service professionals invested much of their time and energy in satisfying customers who should not have been sold MicroTech's products in the first place. The result was much internal feuding and stress.

- His obsession with increasing sales revenues had robbed the company of the resources it needed to lay a foundation for future success. Insufficient time had been spent developing employee talent, improving the computer system, and so on.

- Without guidelines for decision makers, the company operated in reaction mode. Most decisions about where to invest, where to direct marketing efforts, and what criteria to use in hiring new people were based solely upon the profitability of the previous quarter.

- Frank and the management team together developed their "to-be" map, or how they wanted the company to function in the future, which is represented in Figure 5-5.

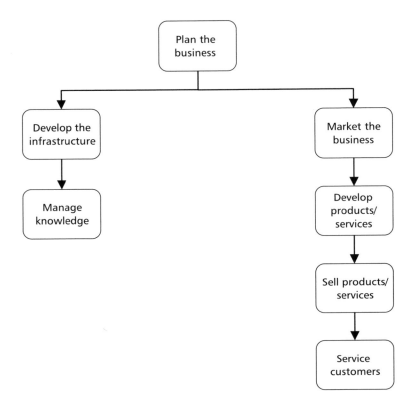

Figure 5-5: MicroTech's "To-Be" Map

As they reflected on the new map, Frank and his management team began to understand the changes that were in store for them and the company.

Leadership Implications

- Each manager had been concerned with the performance of his or her functional area. No one had consciously focused on or felt responsible for critical cross-functional processes. Operating interdependently would now be a critical success factor for company success.
- The managers understood that they would be required to work together in new and unfamiliar ways. And they won-

dered if they could meet the new expectations. No longer would it be sufficient to evaluate their performance by narrow results in their functional areas. New cross-functional measures were required.

- Some managers believed their job was to delegate responsibilities, answer questions, allocate resources, and evaluate performance. Were they equipped to do more strategic thinking, become skilled project managers, supervise total quality management, and deal skillfully with people they did not manage?

Organization Implications

- Significant communication and training will be required for employees to understand the new organization and to operate within the new environment.
- The organization should be organized around several of the major functions. For example, sales, engineering, and customer service employees should participate in establishing product road maps.
- Greater discipline throughout the organization will be required. Individuals must understand that planning is a significant aspect of their jobs. Salespeople should sell only those products approved by marketing. Training and development must be important in good times and bad.
- Taking new approaches to the work may affect short-term revenues.

The new enterprise map had a profound impact on Frank and the members of his leadership group. Frank spent many months questioning his ability to move the organization forward.

Process Definition Overview

A process is a definable, repeatable, measurable activity that produces a clearly defined business result. The map of linked processes shows a view of the organization that is different from the traditional organization chart. A generic process map appears in Figure 5-6.

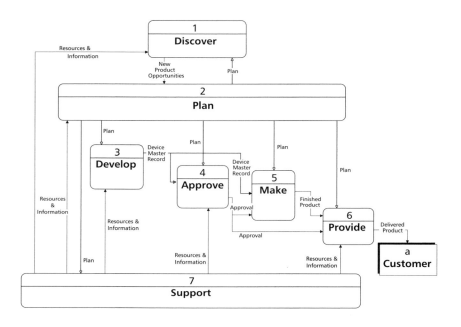

Figure 5-6: Example of Process Map

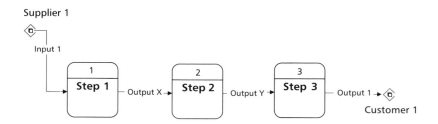

Figure 5-7: High-Level Processes Broken Down into Their Component Parts

Each of the processes above can be further broken down into lower-level processes, as shown in Figure 5-7. The format for an enterprise map requires disciplined use of the language:

Input   Noun
Process name   Verb + noun
Output   Noun

Avoid using the enterprise map of another company as a template because each organization has different requirements. Leaders determine how they want to run the company.

Exercise: Developing Your Enterprise Map

Purpose: To develop an "as-is" and "to-be" enterprise map

Step 1   Assemble the leadership group. Ask others who have been trained in quality management principles to join the group.

Step 2   Explain that the output of this exercise is the identification and clarification of the five to eight processes most critical to the organization. We will use the results to create a picture of how the organization currently operates and how it should operate in the future.

Step 3   Give each person in the group a stack of Post-it® notes. Instruct them to identify all the process elements and major tasks that are performed—one per Post-it® note. Each process/task is to be identified by a verb and noun (for example, pay bills, hire employees, and make sales presentation). Participants complete this exercise in silence. (Talking is likely to reduce the quality and diversity of responses.)

Step 4   Collect all the completed Post-it® notes and randomly place them on a wall.

Step 5   Instruct the group to organize the Post-it® notes into columns of processes that appear to fit together. Members should feel free to shift Post-it® notes. Ask the group to complete this exercise in silence.

Step 6   Ask the group to label each of the columns by giving it a process name. Once again, the verb/noun format should be followed. The process name headers will represent what the group currently sees as the major processes of the organization.

Step 7   Ask the group the following questions:
- Have we identified all the major processes that are required to make our organization more successful?
- Are there any process headers that are not major processes?

Step 8   Write the major process headings on another Post-it® note, being sure to keep the original work intact for now. Organize the processes into a flow that represents how we currently run the business. Ask the following questions:
- Why do we operate the business in this way?
- What are the benefits and the problems of doing so?

Step 9   Create the "to be" enterprise map. Rewrite the process headers on another set of Post-it® notes, preferably of a different color. Ask participants to identify process elements that might be missing, but would be required to improve the organization. Then ask participants to individually develop ways that these processes would fit together. When everyone has finished, ask each person to tell a story about how his or her enterprise map would work.

Step 10   The group decides which of the presented enterprise maps best describes how the organization should work. If the group is dissatisfied with the maps presented, it should work together to develop the optimum solution.

Step 11   Ask the group the following questions:
- What are the major differences/benefits of operating in the new enterprise map?
- What are the implications for leadership of moving in the new direction?
- What are the implications for employees of moving in the new direction?
- What are the major objectives that have to be accomplished to move the organization in the direction of the new enterprise map?

- Do we believe that the benefits of the new enterprise map are worth the effort required to move us in that direction?
- Are we committed to making the necessary changes?

Role Changes

Significant changes in roles are likely to follow shifts in strategy, structure, and process. For example, the accountant who was asked to establish the budget and ensure compliance with it may now have to help process teams develop new measures and methods of capturing critical data. The manager who is used to delegating responsibility may now have to learn to mentor. The salesperson who was skilled at closing deals may need to learn to manage accounts. Because employees may work for the same boss, have the same job title, telephone number, and work space—their new role expectations may be difficult for them to comprehend. Because the leaders will experience many new demands, they too should be prepared to articulate new job requirements to the employees. Leaders may also observe that a few of the employees, who were competent in their old roles, may not be suited to their new roles.

Susan worked for a software company that developed, marketed, and sold enterprise-wide data systems since the early days of its founding. Her particular strengths were sales and establishing strategic partnerships with key vendors. Though her style was autocratic, her business results were extraordinary. The relationship problems she created were overlooked. As the organization and the industry matured, the ability of people to work together more effectively became more critical. Susan's driving style soon became an impediment to the company's further success. Senior management decided that if Susan's ability to work with others did not improve, they would have grounds for termination. At first Susan resented being singled out and criticized for her inability to work effectively with others. She felt abandoned by the managers who had rewarded her performance in the past. With the assistance of a personal coach, Susan began to understand why many of her old behaviors were no longer acceptable. In her mind, she had to learn to achieve business results and to work with people she considered

Table 5-6: From Traditional Role to New Role

Traditional Role	New Role
Responsibilities are fairly well defined in a job description.	Job responsibilities are negotiated as circumstances change.
Leaders are expected to take most of the risk.	Risk is shared with employees.
Technical and professional excellence are prized.	Technical and professional excellence are an entrance requirement; greater emphasis is placed on business and interpersonal skills.
Most work is completed within the functional group.	Work is split between fulfilling functional and cross-functional responsibilities.
Employees seek clarity around expectations.	Employees cope with ambiguity as business opportunities arise.
Employees are responsible for the completion of a task.	All are responsible for completing tasks in a manner that incorporates the needs of other task holders.

less than competent. Table 5-6 highlights typical role changes that accompany changes in strategy, structure, and processes.

In the traditional hierarchical structure, roles were narrowly and completely described in order to avoid conflict. It was assumed that specialists in functional areas had superior knowledge and judgment. Given the complexity of the market environment, the demand for performance from employees is much greater than in times past. Consequently, the role of the leader is much more fluid. Sometimes the leader is the prime mover for strategic thought, sometimes the coach, sometimes a follower, sometimes an architect of the community, and sometimes the one who must wrestle with critical and controversial issues.

Followers are more likely to change if leaders alter their behavior. In the Introduction to this book, we asked you to review your calendar to determine where you were spending your time. Perhaps at this point you have broadened your understanding of

Table 5-7: Alternate Leadership Roles and Definitions of Work

Role Name	Definition of Work
Vessel holder	Maintains an environment of open exploration, curiosity, reflection; encourages people to ask and stay with the difficult problems rather than move toward quick, ineffective solutions
Protector	Maintains psychological safety, upholds guidelines and values of the community
Navigator	Guides the group through processes to achieve results, suggests possible direction and helps to overcome hurdles along the way
Learning facilitator	Poses issues or questions for consideration; models learning by reflecting and commenting on the learning process itself
Evocateur	Sees and asks "What's needed, what's missing, what has not been said?" Raises issues and inconsistencies, draws out members and encourages them to risk speaking the truth
Jester	Through humor creates an environment for learning and dealing with paradoxes
Guide	Experienced traveler who can take the whole group through difficult times

Adapted from Gozdz, 1995: p. 252.

the leadership challenges. Listed above are examples of the roles that a leader of a developing workplace community can play. Compare the list you generated with the possible roles in Table 5-7. What changes in your role may be appropriate?

Exercise: Determine Your Community Leadership Role

Purpose: Results are most effective when the leaders of the organization work together to help clarify the functional leadership responsibilities required to move the organization toward achieving its vision.

Step 1   Ask what people in your organization like about how they are being led. Based on that assessment, which of the management roles are executed well by the leadership function?

Step 2   As you review your core strategy, what implications do you see for leaders' roles? Of the list of potential leader roles, which will be more critical in the future?

Step 3   Once the group has agreed on the critical new roles or those that should be strengthened, describe the behavior and impact those roles might have on the company.

Step 4   Determine which leaders will take on which new roles. More than one person can assume a role.

Step 5   The senior leader will take on the role of helping vessel holder, to help the leaders adopt their roles and achieve the results that were articulated in Step 3. Periodically, the leaders should devote meeting time to evaluating their role behaviors and the progress they have made.

Organizational Learning

Organizations that identify themselves with specific products limit their opportunities for growth. In time, it will be easy for a competitor to match current products and services and deliver superior ones. It is much more difficult for competitors to imitate the competencies of individuals in critical functions or the capabilities of the business. An organization's competence consists of several processes linked together in unique ways. Strategic vision and competence go hand in hand. If an organization lacks a critical competence, it must decide whether to outsource the processes or develop the competence. Competence is typically not developed by one function alone. Consistent with the theme of this chapter, diverse people working intently together typically develop two to four organization competencies that are critical to growing the business. Competencies are the responsibility of the leadership group. Competencies not only become the key barriers to the competition; they are essential to reinventing the business in reframing the future. Table 5-8 provides examples of key organizational competencies.

Table 5-8: Examples of Organizational Competencies

Company	*Competency*
Telemarketing	• Information system linking customer buying habits with specific products, lead management system • Telesales/marketing capabilities • Ability to find fresh/high quality products • Ability to partner with vendors
Microchip testing device manufacturer	• In-depth knowledge of microcircuit testing industry • Ability to manufacture a product with unique materials critical to the industry • In-depth knowledge of each customer's test floor available to sales, engineering, and service employees
Residential real estate company	• High-quality agent development activities • Access to significant reserves of cash for mortgages • National and international affiliations with other real estate organizations

Exercise: Determining the Critical Competencies of Your Organization

During the latter part of the '90s, a common trend has been to outsource processes that are not central to the long-term success of the business and to upgrade competencies that are central to its core.

The purpose of this exercise is to identify existing and/or required organizational competencies, to achieve the vision defined in the core strategy.

Step 1 **Preparing to do the work**

Assemble a group of employees who represent a broad spectrum of management within the organization. Explain that they are there to identify the critical competencies that have enabled past success and to identify those organizational competencies required for future growth. Explain that competence here does not refer to the effectiveness of one segment of the organization or assets of the corporation. It is an ability of several departments or even of linkages with outside organizations that enable the company to achieve superiority in its marketplace.

Step 2   **Determining the competencies**

Ask the group the following questions:
- What organizational skills do we need to possess to excel in the market, that is, to reframe our future?
- If we were to reduce the list of organizational skills to the top two or three, what would they be?
- Are these sufficient to drive our success? If not, then we have not yet identified the essential competencies.

Step 3   **Determining if we have identified the right competencies**

To determine if we have defined the essential organizational competencies, we must address the following questions:
- Will the identified competencies add significant customer value in the future?
- Have the critical elements of the essential competencies been identified?
- Do the competencies span the work of several departments?
- How do we *know* that we excel at this core competence?
- Were a broad number of participants involved in the determination of the competencies?

Step 4   **Next steps**
- What do we need to do to improve existing competencies?
- What do we need to do to develop those competencies that we do not currently possess?
- How will we clearly communicate our core competence to critical stakeholders to improve sales, employee development efforts, and so on?

Learning to Learn

Leaders encourage employees to critically examine their workplace, key relationships, sense of self, and notion of accomplishment. To do so requires understanding how the organization's parts fit together to form the whole, what works, and what needs repair. It requires the ability to make judgments without being judgmental, to let go of ideas and behaviors that are no longer useful.

Learning is hard because we want to do things perfectly. We fear that if we make mistakes, we will look foolish. However, the need to be perfect colors our ability to hear the truth, or to comprehend that what might have been right in the past may no longer be so. Unlearning may be essential to future success. Learning new behaviors requires slowing down long enough to listen and try. We feel we already have too much on our plate, and slowing down would be a luxury. Seldom viewed as opportunities, issues are seen as hot potatoes—no one wants to be holding them. Leaders can use two approaches in meetings to develop a comprehensive understanding of the issues and to ensure the discontinuance of recurring problems.

After Action Review

Groups need to review their interactions so that they can change their behavior. The United States Army's After Action Review has great applicability to the workplace. The skill to use the review process in a consistent manner takes time and practice to develop. The After Action Review is particularly suited to situations in which people have not worked together effectively to solve a problem or complete a project.

- What was supposed to happen?
- What did happen?
- What should we do about it now?
- How can we take what we have learned and apply it in the future?

Exercise: Working Through an Autopsy

Purpose: To more fully learn from a successful or unsuccessful group experience

Step 1   Look for a recurring problem with a group who typically must work together. Involve people who value introspection. Invite all key individuals to participate in order to ensure attendance. At first it may be helpful to choose a simple issue to facilitate learning the review process.

Step 2   Ask people to gather as much information about the issue/problem as possible before coming together as a group. Ask them to answer the standard journalistic questions: Who? What? Where? When? How?

Step 3   The facilitator should describe the issue to be addressed and mention that this is to be a learning session. In order to ensure honest conversation, norms are created for the meeting. Examples of appropriate meeting norms in this situation include:

- Speak truth, as we know it.
- There will be no negative repercussions for speaking up.
- Listen to one another and learn; do not pass judgment; there is no blame.
- Use new learning and insight to improve the organization.
- Everyone participates.

Step 4   After some discussion, the facilitator asks the group, "What was supposed to happen?" People describe in detail what they believe was supposed to have occurred. The facilitators encourage participants to articulate unspoken assumptions.

Step 5   The facilitator asks the group, "What actually happened?" Using the information from Step 2, the group reconstructs in detail the events as they unfolded. The facilitator, after asking the group if all the relevant information has been put forth, concludes this step.

Step 6   The group spends a significant amount of time discussing and learning from the events. Sample questions are:

- Were role and task expectations appropriately communicated at the beginning?
- Where did the breakdowns occur?
- How did we communicate with each other when our expectations were unfulfilled?
- What capabilities should we have had to do this better?
- What happened because things did not go according to plan?
- When things did not go according to plan, what were the results?
- What could each person in the room have done to establish better results?

Step 7   The facilitator restates the purpose of the session and asks:

- What future events may we find ourselves in that are similar?
- What will each of us do differently next time?
- What impact might this have on how we do business?
- How can we communicate what we have learned to others?

Adapted from Sullivan, 1996: pp. 195–201

Measures and Systems

Imagine driving an automobile, unable to see through the windshield, content to focus only on the odometer as a means of evaluating progress. As preposterous as such a technique sounds, leaders do the same when they use financial performance as their primary means for evaluating organizational success. Current financial results, which represent past decisions, are unlikely to predict the future. The focus on financial indicators overemphasizes short-term decision making at the expense of the long-term health of the organization. Leaders need specific performance and outcome measures to know how to improve the organization and where to focus employee efforts. Effective measures are tied to the core strategy. They specify what will be accomplished and how. Table 5-9 describes four kinds of measures that, when used together, encourage a balanced approach.

Table 5-9: Examples of Core Measurements and Their Purposes

Core Measurement Area	Purpose	Examples of Measures
Customer satisfaction	To specify what must be delivered to meet/exceed customer expectations. To discover how well the organization is doing	Market share Customer retention Customer acquisition Customer satisfaction Customer profitability
Process	To reduce the time requirements, improve quality, reduce costs, and innovate methods by which products are produced and delivered	Percent of new product sales Level of scrap/rework Waiting time between process steps Performance against benchmarks
Learning	To specify needed employee competencies	Employee satisfaction and retention Revenue per employee Assessment of core competencies
Financial	To link measures increase revenues, decrease costs, improve productivity, and enhance asset utilization	Revenue Cost reduction/productivity improvement Improve working capital

Adapted from Kaplan, 1996.

When organized and reviewed, the measures should tell a comprehensive story. For example, Company A has decided that it must readjust its strategy to maintain its long-term competitive advantage in the market place. To do so requires that employees learn new skills and that the organization acquire and refine several core competencies. Improvement in key processes is designed to increase productivity, decrease product delivery cycles, and increase customer satisfaction.

Exercise: Develop Balanced Scorecard Measures for Your Organization

Purpose: This exercise should be completed after the core strategy for the organization has been determined and developed. It is designed to ensure that the measures of organizational success are tied to the strategy of the organization.

Step 1   Assemble the key leaders and managers. Include people who may not have had the opportunity to participate in the development of the core strategy. List the benefits of using the balanced scorecard. Explain how the process will assist in achieving the core strategy.

Step 2   For each of the objectives within the core strategy, develop measures, ensuring an appropriate balance among the four measurement areas.

Step 3   For each of the selected measures, develop the information required to accurately produce it. Understand how the measures interrelate and affect one another.

Step 4   Develop a plan to achieve the objectives by using good project management approaches.

Step 5   Develop a communications plan.

Systems

Communities require transportation, sewer, educational, and government systems. Without them, people could not effectively live or work together. Organizations require people, information, and financial systems to ensure that the people and financial resources are aligned to achieve the vision and mission. They ensure that each individual:

- Knows how they will contribute to the whole
- Possesses the necessary information to perform his or her responsibilities
- Has the resources to accomplish his or her responsibilities
- Receives feedback to know how his or her efforts have made a difference

Performance Management

The performance appraisal process has been inadequate for establishing mutual expectations. Because it was designed as a process primarily to establish salary changes, most leaders are dissatisfied with the outcomes of appraisal discussions. Realizing the inadequacy of the process, leaders spend significant time reformatting their forms—to no avail. If the outcome of achieving a stronger bond with the employee is to be established, a new paradigm is required. Table 5-10 provides a comparison of the common performance evaluation process and a performance management process.

Within the performance management process, the employee and the leader review the core strategy and other critical objectives. They determine what will be accomplished. This forms the basis of a performance plan for a period of time. At the end of the period, the employee and the leader review performance and establish a new performance plan as well as the organizational support to achieve it. This process reduces the level of subjectivity in performance evaluation and empowers employees to participate in a meaningful fashion. Training in how to establish, monitor, and evaluate performance should be provided to managers and employees. Performance management is most effective when the process is sponsored, implemented, and tested at the senior levels of the organization.

Table 5-10: Comparison of Performance Appraisal and Performance Management

	Performance Appraisal	*Performance Management*
Perspective	95% past, 5% future	90% future, 10% past
Integration with other processes	Only HR programs, such as compensation	Strategic and departmental planning Strategic and departmental review Compensation
Primary reason for completing	To obtain a merit increase for the employee through the Human Resources Department	To determine the work that needs to be performed To develop a development plan To make a salary determination
Role of the employee	To have performance judged	To assist in determining the work To take primary responsibility for professional development To document changes
Role of the manager	To judge performance To document the exchange	To estimate competency To contribute to the final document
Compensation decisions	Based on nebulous criteria, typically very subjective	Based on the contract established at the beginning of the period, still somewhat subjective
Frequency	Once per year	At least every six months and upon achievement of significant milestones
Relationship between manager and the employee	Boss/subordinate	Partnership to encourage future performance and establish accountability

Computer Systems

Long-term and strategic business interests are enabled via the installation of new technology. Leaders have begun using enterprise models; that is, they integrate operating data from various parts of the organization to develop a picture of the whole organization. The availability of the enterprise model and the data requires employees to know what measures are important, how to interpret the information provided, and how to integrate their work efforts across functions and processes. Thus, leaders provide employees with the means to move from a task orientation, to using data to manage their value-adding contributions.

As organizations move from a focus on product to a focus on product/service mix, employees must gain greater understanding of customer needs, and develop feedback from customers when they use the product. For example, a tractor manufacturer placed sensors on tractors to assess soil conditions and productivity. These measures are taken while the tractor operates in the field. The data are sent via satellite for computer analysis. The data are then made available to agronomists who assist the farmer, again via satellite, in making decisions. The tractor company has expanded its core competence from manufacturing and producing a product to providing a real-time service by managing the collection and use of knowledge.

As organizations grow, leaders establish the means for collective intelligence. They ensure that people come together and share ideas, coordinate the work, and assess progress against goals.

Summary

Leaders ask people to become more collaborative, responsive, flexible, and so on in order to make the business successful. In return, leaders provide an environment where people make a difference, establish a sense of belonging, and do meaningful work.

Community exists when people commit to organizational success, share common processes and best practices, identify with team relationships, and depend on one another for support and collaboration. Community leaders help people with diverse responsibilities and skills to work together, establish an extraordinary level of trust, create flexible organizational boundaries, and operate in diverse geographical locations.

The essential building blocks of workplace community include the following:

1. Building a leadership team and function to ensure that no single person becomes a constraint to organization success
2. Establishing the strategy, vision, mission, values, and objectives of the organization
3. Establishing an organizational structure that is consistent with the core strategy of the organization
4. Understanding and improving the processes that cross traditional functional organizational boundaries
5. Defining new employee roles that align with changes in strategy, structure, and process
6. Determining core competencies to execute the strategy
7. Establishing a mix of measures that allow employees to understand what must be accomplished and how their contributions will be evaluated
8. Developing personnel, information, and financial systems to ensure that people know what to accomplish and have the financial resources available to support their efforts.

Building workplace community is perhaps the most difficult of the five challenges to implement because of the number of people and the level of complexity involved. Appendix B describes employee communications methods for each phase of community building.

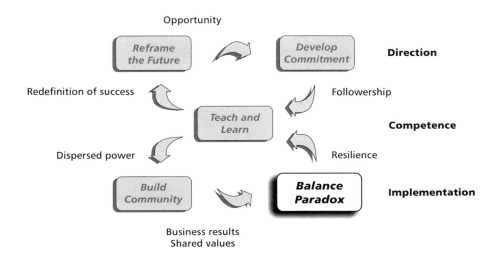

Opportunity

Reframe the Future

Develop Commitment

Direction

Redefinition of success

Followership

Teach and Learn

Competence

Dispersed power

Resilience

Build Community

Balance Paradox

Implementation

Business results
Shared values

CHAPTER 6

Balance Paradox

It would take a poet of Shakespearean dimension to do justice to the extraordinary, maddening, visionary, and debilitating personality of Richard Nixon—at once thoughtful and quirky, compassionate, and insensitive; sometimes fiercely loyal, at other times leaving old associates in his wake as casualties. Yet ultimately Nixon's obvious and unending struggle with himself proved unsettling, even threatening, because deep down one could never be certain that what one found so disturbing in Nixon might not also be a reflection of some suppressed flaw in oneself.

—Henry Kissinger

David is in a bind. He once believed that leadership was about establishing a plan and following it. As a superb salesperson and branch manager, his approach had worked perfectly. Then David was promoted to CEO. Last year, a consulting firm helped him create a strategic plan. At the conclusion of the process, the planners heartily agreed that the decision to move from being a product and service business to providing a broad set of services was indeed a brilliant strategy. This year, he faces the consequences of that decision. The part of the business that can easily move in the new direction represents only 20 percent of revenues. Because it is in the early stages of development, it operates unprofitably. The traditional business represents the balance of revenues and operates extremely profitably. If David were to force the whole organization to move in the new direction, he would risk alienating the majority of employees and decimate short-term profits. If he were to ignore the plan and operate the organization as it was in the past, he would risk the long-term health of the business.

Purpose

David is living in the midst of an organizational dilemma, or paradox. A paradox is a seemingly impossible combination of ideas or actions. Because of their contradictory nature, paradoxes cannot be solved—they must be lived through. Logical definitions, however, cannot convey the torment, pain, confusion, and challenge that result from the dilemmas presented by paradoxes. David feels trapped. He feels that he must pick a single course of action, which alone will not provide a satisfactory response. As a result, he feels that he is in a box or "damned if I do and damned if I don't." In the midst of the absurdity of paradox, anyone is likely to feel trapped, alone, inadequate, and vulnerable. Although paradox is very much a part of the fabric of life, we generally think that we are the only ones to experience its pain and frustration. Fortunately, the outcome of paradox is often positive. When we see a paradox through to the other side, we are likely to be wiser and better able to understand the richness and the complexity of life.

David, like all leaders who are taking their organizations through change, is trying to move his organization in the right direction. He meets an unexpected and unresolvable issue. If David does not manage this particular paradox, his business will not survive. Working through paradox will require contemplation, courage, and understanding. In working through the issues, David is unlikely to find a simple answer or a straightforward agenda. He is learning that leadership is more than creating a plan and crossing off objectives as they are accomplished. He now understands that no single solution drives success. Rather he must balance the short-term capabilities of his company with its long-term goals. Perhaps there is room for the traditional business and the new. His job will be to persuade the organization to accept that both positions have value.

In this chapter, we will explore how paradoxes arise, the elements of a paradox, the distinction between a paradox and a problem, and tools for addressing each.

Paradoxes Are Not Problems

Most of us assume that if we sufficiently analyze a problematic situation, we will come up with a single best solution. Then, when that solution doesn't work, we will assume that we made the wrong decision. We will revisit the issue to find a better answer. When our problem-solving approach doesn't work we will berate ourselves.

As David found, no single course of action will achieve the intended result. Leaders differentiate between issues that can be solved and issues that must be balanced. Problems are likely to have a single best solution and are resolvable, whereas paradoxes have no solution. The comparison is illustrated in Figure 6-1.

When leaders treat paradoxes as if they were problems, they experience the following consequences:

- They find limited success with their solutions and must revisit the issues.

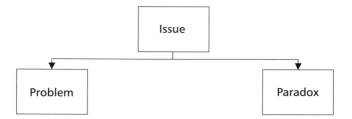

Figure 6-1: Problem vs. Paradox

- They create additional problems or intensify paradoxes.
- They treat people as if they had personality problems.

Two questions distinguish between problems and paradoxes:

1. Is this situation ongoing?
2. Are there two poles that must be simultaneously managed?

Use the questions in Table 6-1 to determine if you are dealing with a problem or a paradox.

Exercise: Understanding Paradox Part 1

In this chapter, we ask you to identify issues, determine which are problems and which are paradoxes, and select one to further understand. We also provide tools for insight and for discovering an appropriate course of action.

Purpose: To determine which issues are problems and which are paradoxes and to learn how to balance a paradox

Step 1   List the issues. Include issues faced by the organization or by you as you execute the responsibilities of your leadership position.

Step 2   Use the two questions above to determine whether the issues are problems or paradoxes.

Table 6-1: Distinguishing Problem from Paradox

Problem	*Paradox*
Issue 1	
This is a new issue.	We have tried a number of solutions for this issue, and nothing seems to work.
Issue 2	
There are no interdependent poles to be managed.	Both sides of the issue seem to have validity.
Examples	
• Are we in this business or that business?	• Do we focus on a core business or a new one?
• How do we reduce costs?	• Are we customer-, employee-, or technology-focused?
• Which one do we purchase?	• Do we assume a rational, an intuitive, or an emotional perspective on this issue?

Adapted from Johnson, 1996.

How Leaders Experience Paradox

Paradoxes exist at three levels: organizational, role, and individual.

Organizational Paradox

Leaders understand the need to manage the competing interests of such organizational stakeholders, as owners, employees, suppliers, and customers. What may be in the best interest of one stakeholder may not be in the best interest of another. Organizational leadership requires making choices that seem to be mutually exclusive. Do we:

- Focus on making short-term profits or ensure the long-term health of the company?

- Decentralize resources to improve service delivery or centralize them to reduce costs?
- Reward team and group effort or reward outstanding individual performance?
- Grow quickly to take advantage of current market opportunities or grow slowly to ensure that we have the infrastructure to support our growing number of customers?
- Maintain a high profile when an embarrassing issue emerges or maintain a low profile, hoping that no one will notice?
- Honor the needs of loyal employees who prefer a stable working environment or focus on constantly changing customer demands?
- Encourage a corporate culture that focuses on tasks or one that focuses on processes?

Role Paradox

Although job descriptions may precisely define leader accountabilities, in reality, leadership paradoxes can seldom be spelled out and comprehended. Leaders are supposed to:

- Listen to employees, but not be wishy-washy in making decisions
- Communicate openly, but not damage others with their communications
- Provide honest feedback, but not bruise people's feelings
- Be in charge of what is going on, but not micromanage
- Empower others to decide what to do, but not abandon those who prefer to be told what to do
- Be totally competent, but not be closed to learning

Individual Paradox

Characteristics that allow a leader to appear competent in one setting may be perceived as weaknesses in another. The following are examples of frequently observed personal paradoxes:

- Being flexible can help us deal with changing times and can cause us to be seen as wishy-washy.

- Being opinionated means having the conviction to make things happen and being perceived as not listening to others.
- Being able to see the big picture and far into the future indicates that we may easily do strategic planning and not so easily implement short-term plans.
- Wanting to be a strong leader of an organization and fearing conflict
- Having excellent analytical skills and poor human relationships skills
- Having very strong opinions about how things should be and fearing alienating others

An Example of the Three Levels of Paradox

Mary, the editor of a successful metropolitan newspaper, sees herself as someone who is uncomfortable around most people. She also sees herself as highly analytical. She prefers to solve problems and tell people what to do. She has sufficient insight to know that her interpersonal style interferes with her goal of becoming a great leader. She claims two professional agendas. First, she wants the newspaper to become part of the glue that holds the community together; she hopes to develop the "shared life of the community." Second, she wants to provide a less stressful work environment.

Newspapers have formats, characters, philosophies, and points of view that shape decisions. To become an instrument for weaving the fabric of the community together, a newspaper has to acknowledge and address controversy. Bringing out conflict and encouraging dialogue can help to cement a community together; they can also provide the friction to tear it apart. Editors are seldom viewed as neutral parties. Their process of bringing issues to the forefront also brings editors into the center of controversies in the community. But Mary is a shy woman. She avoids the public eye. Simultaneously, her professional role casts her into the center of community conflicts.

Mary is responsible for ensuring a high-quality work environment. She finds it personally and professionally upsetting to see her employees suffer stress as the result of pressures that are inherent in the traditional organizational structure that past leaders put into place to produce the newspaper. Mary realizes that she has to change the organizational structure to one that is more team-based. Mary also realizes that she has to change her leadership style. She must become more strategically oriented than problem-oriented. She must help people learn how to solve their problems, rather than solving problems for them. Most important, she has to create forums for change. Only recently did she become aware that she is part of the problem and part of the solution.

These revelations create private difficulties for Mary. She has to become more visible to employees, something that she would rather avoid. She may have to admit that she does not have the answers to complex problems. For a person who perceives herself to be a strong and successful professional, perhaps the greatest paradox lies in finding that she lacks the capacity to achieve her professional interests.

Mary's situation demonstrates the three levels of paradox. At the level of the organization, the process of binding the organization together may foment the arguments that could tear it apart. At the role level, paradox lies in helping to reduce the level of stress in the organization, and knowing that changing the structure will temporarily increase the level of stress. The personal paradox is that a leader who prefers to solve tactical problems must step back and become more strategic.

Exercise: Understanding Paradox Part 2

Purpose: Earlier in this chapter, you listed the issues you face and determined whether they are problems to be solved or paradoxes to be managed. In Part 2 of the exercise, you will determine whether the paradoxes you face are at the organization, role, or individual level.

Step 1   Refer to the list of issues in Part 1 of this exercise earlier in the chapter.

Step 2   For each paradox, note whether it is organizational, role, or individual.

Step 3   Determine one paradox to work with as you complete this chapter.

Major Components of a Paradox

All paradoxes contain polarities. That is, they have two aspects that appear opposite to each other. Typically one side is more strongly preferred than the other. For example, team versus individual, centralized versus decentralized, and so on. Paradoxes are perceived through sets of unarticulated and unrecognized assumptions. To better understand a paradox, one must recognize both poles and state one's assumptions so that they can be appropriately challenged. The leader must ensure that both sides of a paradox are appropriately addressed.

It's Not One or the Other...It's Both

Many leaders in Mary's situation would be tempted to use the scientific method: Define the problem, develop a hypothesis, look for alternate solutions, choose the most promising course of action, implement it, and hope for the best. They learned this method in school. In most corporate settings, problem solving is highly rewarded. The underlying assumption that a best course of action must exist is clearly not the case in Mary's situation. Mary must challenge her organization to meet the vision and the mission of the company; to do otherwise would mean to risk languishing in mediocrity.

At the core of most paradoxes is the reality of two contradicting forces—it's not one or the other...it's both. Mary must pursue her professional responsibilities knowing that she may not succeed. Like other leaders, she must focus on the short term and the long term. She must listen and be resolute. She must have answers and be open to learning. Unfortunately, most of her professional preparation has focused on how to solve problems, not on how to balance paradoxes. Her first step, then, is to identify the paradoxes and the polarities embedded in them.

Polarities may be experienced in degrees along a continuum. Some polarities are experienced in extremes, others are experienced more mildly. The example in Figure 6-2, a paradox of team vs. individual performance, makes this point.

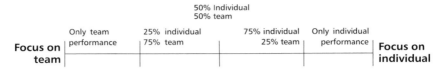

Figure 6-2: Team vs. Individual Polarity

In organizations facing the team versus individual paradox, people will fall throughout the continuum. Rewards may fall at either end of the polarity. For example, focusing only on teamwork means that many individuals will not contribute their best work. Focusing only on individual rewards means that the ability of people to work together may be compromised. Note that a 50/50 split may not be the appropriate course of action. That is compromise, not managing the polarity.

Exercise: Understanding Paradox Part 3

In Part 3 you will identify the poles of the team/individual paradox and the degree to which they are currently being experienced. The example in Figure 6-3 illustrates a completed example of this portion of the exercise.

Step 1   Draw a straight horizontal line, and identify the two ends of the organizational paradox you selected in Part 2 of this exercise. Draw a point at the center of the line.

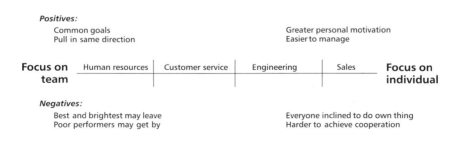

Figure 6-3: Team vs. Individual Polarity by Department

Step 2   At either end of the line, write the extremes of the para-
           dox. Above the line note the positives of each end of the
           polarity. Below the line note the negatives.

Step 3   Locate where you think individuals or departments/func-
           tions are along the line and where they are in positive or
           negative balance.

Paradigms

Humans create internal, unconscious maps of reality, known as
paradigms. Like all maps, paradigms contain information that is
useful in guiding people through life. These maps are, however,
mere representations of reality. They are incomplete and often inaccurate. For example, a friend participated in a bike marathon of
more than 550 miles over five continuous days. As he pored over
the map in anticipation of his journey, he realized that the expected mileage for day three was significantly less than the mileage
for days one and two. He assumed that the organizers wanted to
provide the participants with a respite. He assumed wrong. Day
three was the most grueling day of all. My friend's map indicated
distance and relative location. It did not show topography.

Our maps are based on the teachings of our parents, our life
experiences, and our formal education. Such words as theories,
models, methodologies, principles, assumptions, patterns, common sense, values, frames of reference, traditions, ideologies, and
doctrines describe an order and organization to life (Barker, p. 35).
Our maps "tell us" how the world operates and guide us through
most of the complexities of life.

We use paradigms to help us anticipate order in the world and
reduce our anxieties. Our perception of order provides us with
structure and a sense of comfort. Paradigms are useful to the degree
that they help us solve problems and describe how we should behave. Unfortunately, when our situation changes and issues cannot be resolved through the use of existing mental maps, our paradigms keep us from moving forward because they freeze what we
are able to see and believe. The rule is not only "seeing is believing," but also "seeing what we believe." At the point where our

mental maps no longer fit reality we perceive that we are in a para-doxical situation.

Example of a Paralyzing Paradigm

In the late 1970s and early 1980s, a small company of talented en-gineers created Dicomed Corporation. The company's computers translated satellite transmissions from the moon into graphical images. The company also made the computer stations that graphic designers considered the best in the industry. In the later half of the 1980s, as the computing power of personal computers increased, sales of the graphic design stations began to decline. When revenues faltered, management asked the salespeople why they were unable to achieve their historic levels of revenue. Their answers centered on specific product features and benefits. The salespeople were unable to see the competitive challenge that lay outside their frame of reference. The competitive situation contin-ued to deteriorate, and the company was sold to Crosfield, one of three major players in the prepress market. Crosfield's product line consisted of large scanners driven by large computers. Dicomed's management attempted to avoid their past failures, but their words of prediction and advice fell on the deaf ears of the new owners, who felt that their excellent product would be immune to a similar fate. Within two years, Crosfield was sold to DuPont. Today it is a tiny fraction of its original size.

Old paradigms freeze our ability to pursue new courses of ac-tion. The more successful we have been, the more likely we are to cling to what made us successful. The higher we are in manage-ment, the greater we perceive the risk of trying new practices and the less able we are to let go of old practices. Paradoxically, the less we let go of the past, the more risky our present position actually becomes. Perhaps the senior managers at Crosfield realized that to let go of their understanding of the market meant they would have to admit their own performance failure. Ironically, the engineers at Dicomed soon developed new products based on the power of the personal computer and were eager to partner with Crosfield's engi-neers and salespeople. Unfortunately, their ideas did not coincide with the reason that Crosfield had purchased the company. The lessons learned by Dicomed could not be easily transferred to its new owner.

Inevitably, there comes a time when our paradigms outlive their usefulness. When we hold on to them too long, they become a source of frustration and anxiety rather than a source of comfort. They hold us back from growing and participating fully in the world. Granted, for a time our paradigms are useful in getting us expediently through life, but they limit our perception of the possibilities in new situations. When we realize the disconnection between our paradigms and the reality around us, we will experience emotional confusion and frustration. At such times, we need to determine whether we have a problem to be solved or a paradox that needs to be balanced.

Have you ever wondered why some organizations bounce back after a difficult time and others spiral lower and lower? Why some organizations turn on a dime, while others turn more like aircraft carriers? Partly the answer lies in management's paradigm of the world. The founder's views of the world are passed on to subsequent generations of employees through stories, which have been institutionalized, through corporate strategies, vision statements, and human resources systems. The paradigms of subsequent generations of leaders simply add to the organizational script. As a result, the old paradigm continues to affect decision making until a cataclysmic event necessitates a reality check. When it becomes obvious to some that a new paradigm is required, any change will be met by others with resistance.

Leaders often believe that most issues could be resolved if only they would use the right approach. If they delve into active listening, 360-degree feedback, public speaking, meeting with management, process improvement, and so on, they will be able to persuade people to get the work done and to excel. These approaches can be helpful and can improve people's ability to work together. By themselves, however, they are not useful for resolving paradoxes. Therefore, understanding paradox is critical to leaders who wish to help their organizations become nimble and agile, and anticipate and react to changes in the environment.

Understanding Existing Paradigms in Your Organization

Convincing people that their paradigms of the world are incorrect generally works less well than providing them with the opportunity to express their assumptions. This is an essential ingredient to effectively managing organizational paradoxes. If we review the sample paradox in Part 3 of the above exercise, we find that various functions are likely to perceive various courses of action as more beneficial. Encouraging functional groups to express their views provides insight and allows them to find greater meaning and undergo greater learning. An illustrative example appears in Table 6-2.

Most of us are inclined to discount someone who holds an opposing opinion. Allowing the voices of alternate poles to enter the conversation encourages discussion of the merits of each side of the paradox.

Table 6-2: Team and Individual Performance as Perceived by Different Functions

	About Team Performance	*About Individual Performance*
Sales	Don't see a need to work with others	Work better independently
	Don't want to deal with corporate issues	Will make more money as individuals than as teams
Engineering	Most people outside their area don't understand them	Their technical solution is best for the company
Customer Service	They can solve problems if allowed to work upstream	Individual performance doesn't solve critical interdepartmental issues
Human Resources	May be a way for them to have an impact on the company with new training programs, etc.	Traditional systems geared to focus on individual accomplishment

Table 6-3: Deepen the Understanding of Paradox by Functional Group

Functional Group	One End of Polarity	Other End of Polarity

Exercise: Understanding Paradox Part 4

Purpose: In parts of the exercise completed thus far, you have separated problems from paradoxes, selected a paradox for further consideration, described the positive and negatives of each polarity, and determined how each functional group might fall on a continuum. The next step is to develop a deeper understanding of the paradigm by each functional group. Complete Table 6-3.

Putting It All Together: The Polarity Map™

The purpose of the Polarity Map™, developed by Barry Johnson, is:

- To ensure that we provide proper focus to both ends of the paradox
- To include the voices of people with alternate perspectives
- To create an approach that will yield a long-term solution

A generic Polarity Map™ appears in Figure 6-4. The team versus individual Polarity Map™ appears in Figure 6-5.

Managing the Balance

The key to managing a paradox is to maximize the positive and minimize the negative aspects of both sides. The critical questions that must be answered are:

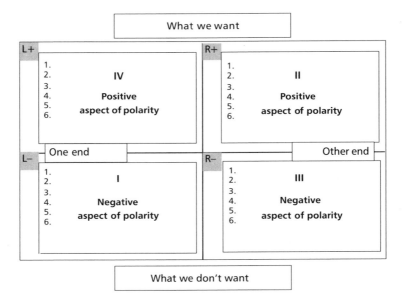

Figure 6-4: **Generic Polarity Map™ (Courtesy of Barry Johnson and Polarity Management)**

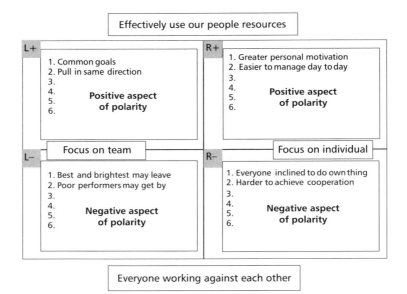

Figure 6-5: **Team vs. Individual Polarity Map™ (Courtesy of Barry Johnson and Polarity Management)**

- What will ensure a dynamic balance between both sides of the paradox?
- How will we know when one side of the paradox dominates?
- Who will do what to manage the balance?

Table 6-4 demonstrates how one team decided to manage the team versus individual paradox.

In the introduction to the chapter, we met David, who discovered the need for his organization to balance the product-driven versus market-driven paradox. Every one of the company's 60-member management group participated in developing the Polarity Map™ in Figure 6–6. Within the few hours it took to complete this exercise, improved healing and understanding developed. Creating the map in Figure 6-6 and Table 6-5 helped people with different perspectives begin to work together.

Table 6-4: Managing the Team vs. Individual Paradox

Team	*Individual*
Managing for positive results: what, who, when	
1. Establish team goals, team leader, 9/30	1. Develop individual goals, team itself, 9/30
2. Develop greater interpersonal skills of members, Human Resources, 2/15	2. Establish career paths, members of team and Human Resources, 1/5
3. Establish team rewards, Human Resources with team leader, 6/15	3. Establish individual rewards, Human Resources and Team Leader, 6/15
The red flag indicators: who will know and what we do about it	
1. All decisions require team consensus, team leader and sponsor—bring up in team	1. Team not making any decisions, team leader—bring up in team meeting
2. Level of conflict is keeping team from performing, team leaders, members—ask coach for help	2. No conflicts are surfacing in meetings despite lack of team performance, team leader—ask for coaching assistance

**Figure 6-6: Market-Driven vs. Product-Driven Polarity Map™
(Courtesy of Barry Johnson and Polarity Management)**

The remainder of this chapter is devoted to further understanding organizational, role, and individual paradoxes.

Organizational Paradox

Leaders typically are perplexed when they learn that employees experience great difficulty in working together. It is not that employees don't have the best interests of the organization at heart; it is that they have different definitions of what is best, based largely upon their educational and professional experiences and the roles they play within the organization.

Figure 6-7 is an internal systems perspective of the organization. It shows the various parts of a typical organization and the

Table 6-5: Product- vs. Market-Driven Action Plan

Product-Driven	Market-Driven
Managing for positive results: what, who, when	
1. Target specific products to improve, service manager, 1/15	1. Learn how to market bundled services
2. Improve targeted products, identified product managers, 8/30	2. Bundle services to make them easier to consume by customers
3. Increase the diversity of products, market managers, 12/30	3. Offer greater diversity of products to specific customers, market leaders, end of year
The red flag indicators: who will know and what we do about it	
1. No stories of working together, market managers, bring to attention of VP marketing	1. Decrease of product quality, VP sales, bring up at executive council
2. Much finger pointing between product lines, any employee to their manager	2. Not developing new products, president, bring up at executive council

mantras of people within each function as they go about their work.

Although these people share a common goal of creating and delivering products and services to the customer, they work with the tensions of interdependence. They also have very different perceptions about who their customer is and what is best for the organization. The marketing department seeks to create product concepts that meet the changing needs of customers. Research and development, which is responsible for taking these concepts and turning them into products, works at odds with the marketing people, whose demands they see as unreasonable. The manufacturing department, who gets the prototypes from the engineering department, is at odds with them when the information comes late or is still too incomplete to produce the product in time to meet the deadlines that have been imposed by the sales department. The sales department, who is charged with selling as much product as

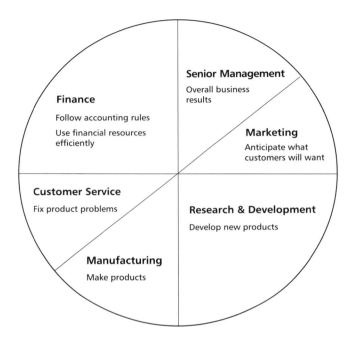

Figure 6-7: Systems View of an Organization

possible, is resented by the customer services department, which must meet installation deadlines and fix the problems that were created by the marketing, engineering, and sales departments.

Cross-functional teams have done much to improve interdepartmental understanding, but the underlying tensions between parts of the business are nevertheless integral to the organization's paradoxes.

Thus an organizational mantra creates a paradigm, a set of assumptions about why a specific function exists. If marketing is responsible for anticipating what customers want, relevant suggestions from engineering will be disregarded or resented by the people in marketing. Thus the marketing paradigm creates a deeply held organizational paradox. Mantras define functional accountabilities, and they limit the function's capacity for interaction within the organization.

Exercise: Understanding Your Organization's Mantras

The following exercise is completed first by the senior leaders and then by other managers. The value of completing this work in teams is that it builds cross-functional organizational understanding.

Purpose: To develop a common understanding of the functional paradigms within the organization and to determine if there are more effective visions for each functional area

Step 1   Ask the people in the group to define what they believe are the functions within the company. A good place to start might be the company's organization chart.

Step 2   Ask each function to develop a slogan that describes their role and/or contribution to the larger organization. Ask the group to define its suppliers and its customers. Create a pie chart similar to the example in Figure 6-7, writing each function's name and slogan.

Step 3   Ask the group to determine problems created by functional mantras. For example, the president might determine that her mantra is, "To ensure that everyone is working together." Taken to its extreme, this could mean that the president feels personally responsible for ensuring that everyone works together, and she might become overly involved in the day-to-day management of the organization.

Step 4   Ask the group to define a reoccurring problem within the organization. Examples might be rising customer complaints, the inability to get product out the door on time, the inability to develop new products, or the failure to share information in a timely fashion. Write the problem on flip chart paper and post it at the front of the room.

Step 5   Create nametags for each represented functional area (marketing, sales, and so on) and ask people to wear them. Ask people to look at the problem on the table from their functional perspective. Typical issues in this analysis might include the following:

1. Given the work that currently exists within this function, how important is the resolution of the issue?
2. From our perspective, the effect that this issue is having on the company is…
3. From our perspective, the cause of the effect is…
4. Our function contributes to or resolves the issue before us as follows…
5. This issue would be resolved if…

Step 6   The group looks at the information, reviews the dynamics of the organization, and considers the implications of not dealing with the issues. Here are several questions that may help the group to process its work:

- What new understanding and insights have we developed about our functional partners?
- How do the good intentions of our department cause problems for another department?
- What are the barriers to resolving the issues?
- How could we communicate and work together more effectively?
- How do our slogans help and hinder organizational progress?
- What other slogans might help us work together more effectively?
- Do we want to use this or a similar process to raise and resolve other issues we are facing?
- How can we extend this learning further into the organization?
- What might be a more effective slogan for each function?
- How could we organize the company more effectively or use our talent more productively?

One variation of the above directions asks people to exchange roles. For example, the marketing person might take on the role of the research and development person, and that individual might take the manufacturing role.

Table 6-6: Examples of Common Organizational Paradoxes

Time:	Focus on the Long Term	or	The Short Term
Strategic direction:	Focus on what made us successful in the past	or	Where we think the future is going
Products:	Deliver a narrow range of products	or	Deliver a broad range of products
Structure:	Centralize	or	Decentralize
Structure:	Organize as a hierarchical structure	or	Organize as a team structure
Communication:	Communicate every-thing and be open	or	Communicate only what is critical
Change:	Remain flexible to changes in the marketplace	or	Focus on what we have done historically
Leadership:	The leaders make most of the decisions	or	Employees share in making most decisions
Values:	We focus on profitability	or	We focus on values
Customers:	We will retain our current customers	or	We acquire new customers

The Organizational Paradox Minefield

A major role of the leadership team is to balance organizational paradoxes. There are many. Left unmanaged, paradoxes can threaten the survival of the organization. Paradoxes are easy to identify because they tend to involve classic themes. Table 6-6 highlights a few such themes.

Exercise: Creating Your Organizational Paradox Minefield

Once leaders understand the fundamentals of paradox, they are ready to create the organizational paradox minefield.

Step 1   Ask the leadership group to list the major issues to be addressed. Narrow the list to a critical five.

Step 2   Determine which of the presenting issues are paradoxes by applying the two questions: Is it a recurring issue? Does it have two polarities (poles) that must be balanced?

Step 3   Build the organization's paradox minefield by creating a large circle. At a point on the outer edge of the circle list one extreme of a paradox; at the opposite point list the other extreme of the paradox.

Step 4   Repeat step three for all organization paradoxes.

Step 5   Through discussion within the group, pinpoint, along each continuum, where the organization is functioning.

Step 6   Determine which paradoxes are most critical to the organization now and in the long term. Determine which seem to be most out of balance and in need of special focus.

Step 7   For each paradox, complete a Polarity Map™ as described above and determine who in the management group will be responsible for balancing the paradox.

The example in Figure 6-8 depicts an organizational paradox minefield. The X's identify where the executive team believed the organization was functioning along each of the four paradoxes. Members of the group had been privately aware that the organization was placing too much emphasis on current product, but no one had raised the issue with the others. The organization had recently moved from a hierarchical structure to one that was more team-based. The discussion helped the leaders understand that if they did not move decision making toward the center of the organization, communication and decision making among the teams could become issues in the future.

Further Thoughts Regarding Organization Paradoxes

1. Most organizations have people who want to pursue a new approach and people who want to maintain the status quo.

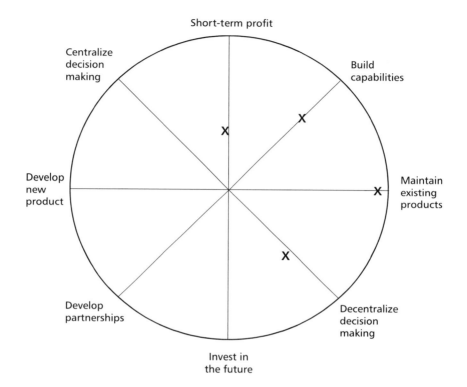

Figure 6-8: Organizational Paradox Minefield

Typically, we perceive the people in the opposite camp as stubborn resisters. Paradox, when it is pursued as above, demonstrates the value of seeing both sides. When people recognize the value of their contributions, their resistance to the new approach diminishes, and changes will have a better chance to succeed.

2. Once the solution to a problem is implemented, the fix can be expected to last a long time. Paradoxes, however, are not static. In the natural ebb and flow between the poles, leadership actions achieve the needed balance. Seldom can we say that a paradox has been fixed for good.

3. For a team-building experience, the leader/facilitator could draw a polarity chart on the floor by using flip chart paper and

ask people to act out the polarity. Acting out a paradox will bring the polarities to the forefront and convince people to work together.

4. For further implementation ideas, read *Polarity Management: Identifying and Managing Unsolvable Problems* by Barry Johnson, 157 Barlow Lake Road, Middleville, MI 49333.

5. It is helpful to create a goal statement about how the leader will balance the paradox. This statement should include the following:

   • What you wish to move from
   • What you want to move toward
   • By when you want to make the change
   • The impact you expect the change to have on the organization
   • What you will do to make the change happen

An example of a goal statement follows:

> "As an organization, we will move from operating by the seat of our pants to working together toward long-term goals. We will implement this change within the next year. We will more precisely choose where we want to remain flexible and thus be able to offer our employees greater stability within the organization. I will begin by establishing a decision-making process around the way we serve specific clients and markets."

Such clarity helps the organization's members work in concert.

Thus far, our focus has been on organizational paradoxes. As individuals execute their role responsibilities they unwittingly encounter role paradox.

Role Paradox

Reva, a Human Resources professional with excellent academic credentials and work experience, had held executive positions in pharmaceutical, software development, and large retail companies.

Despite the differences among the industries in which she worked, Reva found the same role paradoxes in her new job. At first, she thought that the issues came from the way she approached her work or from a personal character flaw. When she commiserated with another Human Resources professional, she learned that the issues she experienced were common.

Human Resources leaders play two roles that are critical to the long-term success of their organizations. First, they must see that company policies and procedures are adhered to. This role requires ensuring compliance with governmental regulations and with performance appraisal and compensation systems. Second, Human Resources professionals must partner with key personnel to develop competent employees and to build organizational capability. Thus, the Human Resources professional appears at times to be a judge and an enforcer of the existing code and at other times to be a coach and developer. Employees who experience the Human Resources professional in these multiple roles may not understand the complexity of his or her responsibilities. They will wonder if they can trust this person to help them meet their own professional agendas. Human Resources executives who overemphasize protecting the organization by focusing on the rules and regulations become ineffective because they are unable to build trust with employees. Those who overemphasize close relationships with employees may be perceived by management as unable to move critical organizational agendas forward. Examples of leader role paradoxes appear in Table 6-7.

Just as leaders and their teams struggle to balance the organization's paradoxes, leaders also privately experience the agony of contradictory role expectations. Many of the tools for dealing with organizational paradox are equally applicable to role paradox. Leaders who tend to be too closely identified with their positions may find it difficult to see the paradoxes of their roles. Working with a coach can be quite useful when sorting through paradoxes. The coach's understanding and use of such tools as the Polarity Map™ will calm us and help us develop the balance we require to deal with our leadership paradoxes.

Table 6-7: Common Examples of Leader Role Paradoxes

Do I focus on the needs of the individual?	or	Do I focus on the needs of the organization?
Do I focus on the needs of my function?	or	Do I focus on the needs of the process or company?
Do I communicate what I know?	or	Do I communicate what I think should be said?
Do I focus on accomplishing specific tasks?	or	Do I focus on getting others to accomplish specific tasks?
Do I focus on the needs of our customers?	or	Do I focus on the needs of the organization?
Do I work to make me look good?	or	Do I work to make others look good?
Do I work hard to be perfect?	or	Do I work at a level to be just good enough?

Suggestions for Handling Role Paradox

If there are significant issues with your role as leader, follow the steps below:

Step 1   List the issues you are facing and determine whether they are:
  1. Problems to be solved
  2. Paradoxes to be managed
  3. Competencies you wish to master

Step 2   For paradoxes to be managed, create a role paradox minefield similar to the organizational minefield noted earlier.
  1. Explain to others what you are trying to accomplish and ask for feedback about where they see you functioning on the map for each of the paradoxes you face and where they believe you might be more effective.
  2. Assess where you are currently functioning and where you believe would be optimal for each of the paradoxes.

3. Determine the one paradox where you wish to achieve a better balance.

Step 3   Create a Polarity Map™ for the paradox.

Step 4   Develop a plan for managing the paradox. You may want to invite your boss, a coach, or a board member to help you develop the plan and monitor its implementation.

Managing Conflict

As people deploy their responsibilities in specific areas of the organization, their interests will collide. Relationships are the critical junction where organizational and functional successes are determined. A conflict of roles is generally experienced as a conflict of goals, resources, time, and quality. For example:

- Departments or functions typically want to deliver a high-quality output. If they take the time to do things perfectly, they risk delaying others who will have less time for doing their part. If they do not do their part correctly, they are criticized for producing an inferior product or service.
- When fulfilling one's responsibilities requires the use of additional resources, there may be insufficient resources for the next person to accomplish his or her responsibilities.
- Entering data in a certain way may simplify the first process job, but this work method may increase the difficulty of obtaining the information needed by someone else.

Typically, when approaching conflict, people feel that they are in a bind and believe that there will be a winner and a loser. The model in Figure 6-9 is particularly helpful in dealing with issues of apparent paradox when the issues revolve around perceptions of scarcity of resources.

The two dimensions of conflict are the degree of personal assertiveness and the degree of cooperation between the parties. Nonconfrontational strategies are associated with avoidance and accommodation. Control-oriented strategies are associated with competition. Solution-oriented approaches are associated with col-

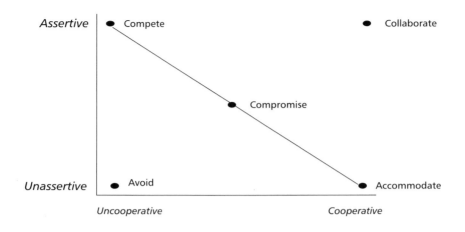

Figure 6-9: Dimensions of Conflict-Handling Orientations (Adapted from Quinn et al, 1995: p. 99)

laboration and compromise. When the perspective is one of scarcity, individual actions will fall in the triangular portion of the graph. When people perceive a world of abundance, their behaviors will fall above the zero-sum line (the diagonal line). Any of the five approaches may be best in particular circumstances, but true collaboration diminishes perceptions of scarcity. Table 6-8 identifies the importance of being flexible.

Exercise: Practice Mapping Your Conflict Strategy

Table 6-8 provides a variety of conflict strategies. Table 6-9 is a worksheet for diagnosing a current conflict. The assumptions behind this conflict model are twofold: (1) the two parties are in disagreement about the proper course of action and (2) the criteria by which to choose a selected conflict-management strategy will depend on:

- How important the issue is to you
- How much power/influence you have in the relationship

Table 6-8: When to Use the Five Conflict Management Approaches

Approach	*Appropriate Situation*
Compete	• Quick decisive action is critical. • Unpopular issues need to be implemented. • Leader is keenly aware of what is right and must move quickly. • Protection against people who may hurt the organization.
Collaborate	• Both individuals have concerns that are too important to be ignored. • The objective is to learn. • There is time to merge insights of people with different perspectives. • Commitment to follow-through is critical. • Feelings have interfered with relationships. • A creative or innovative solution is needed.
Compromise	• Goals are important, but not sufficiently important to disrupt the action. • The individuals have equal power and are committed to mutually exclusive goals. • Temporary settlements for a complex issue are OK. • Under pressure of time an expedient solution is needed. • Collaboration and competition have been unsuccessful.
Avoid	• The issue is trivial. • There is little probability of satisfying your own concerns. • The costs of disruption outweigh the benefits of resolution. • People need time to cool down. • Information for making a decision is not at hand. • The presenting issues seem to be related to another issue.
Accommodate	• Your position is less accurate or useful than the other person's. • The issue is more important to the other person than to you. • You desire to build emotional credits in a relationship account. • You wish to minimize a loss when you are outmatched. • Harmony and stability are important to you. • The other person could learn by making a mistake.

Adapted from Quinn et al, 1995: p. 102.

Table 6-9: Comparing Important Dimensions When Assessing the Conflict Approach

	Me (High, Medium, Low)	*Other Person (High, Medium, Low)*	
Importance of the issue to you			Importance of the issue to the other person
Degree of power/influence you have over the other person			The degree of influence/power the other person has over you
Do you need additional support for your perspective?			Does the other person need additional support?
The relationship with the other person is open and honest.			The other person sees your relationship as open and honest.
The time frame to make the decision is short.			The other party views a similar time frame for making the decision.
It is important that a positive work relationship continue beyond this specific conflict.			It is important for the other person to have a positive relationship with you beyond the initial conflict.

- How much additional support will be required by the other party
- The nature of the relationship between you and the other person
- The time frame in which the decision will have to be made
- The desired long-term outcome of the relationship

- The more important the issue is to you, the more you will want to take an active role. This suggests using a collaborative or competitive approach.
- The more power you have in the relationship, the more you are able to determine the outcome of the conflict. If you have less power, you may opt for the accommodate or withdrawal approach. If you have more power, you may opt for one of the other styles.
- If you need additional support from the other person to accomplish the task, you may wish to take more of a collaborative or an accommodating approach.
- If your relationship is open and honest, it is best to take a collaborative approach to ensure the long-term health of the relationship.
- If the time frame in which to make the decision is short, it is best to take a proactive approach and avoid withdrawing from the situation.
- If it is important to maintain a positive relationship, it is helpful to take a collaborative and open position during the conflict.

Based on the above analysis, which conflict approach best suits this situation? What must you do to be successful? What would happen if you tried an alternate approach? Develop several scenarios before beginning to deal with the situation.

Values in Conflict

When people share a common core of values, they will openly and honestly approach the problems they share. When different values drive their behavior, they will find it difficult to conduct business in a manner that is mutually satisfying.

A Fortune 50 financial services company sought to organize its retail distribution sales organization into small groups of 3 to 6 sales people. The groups were encouraged to participate in business-planning sessions, which offered them the opportunity to discuss their values and to establish the direction of their business. Those groups that developed a set of core values and modeled their behavior accordingly were able to work together to resolve the issues that inevitably arose in the complexities of doing business. For example, people who were primarily focused on the success of the group found it difficult to work with those who were primarily focused on their own success. People who were focused on building the business by supporting the long-term success of their clients often clashed with people who were focused on their own short-term financial success.

If you find that you are in conflict with someone whose core values differ significantly from yours, it is important to bring your value differences to the table. Doing so has a paradoxical effect. Each party to the conflict becomes more honest, each allows for the differences in values, and each will prefer to walk away from the engagement while they remain on speaking terms. It will be sufficient to understand that you may never resolve your differences, but you can agree to disagree.

People resist changing their fundamental values. Only through a life-altering event will they become introspective, take an inventory, and consider keeping or changing the values by which they operate. If you are in conflict with someone who has a different set of values, it makes sense to accept the differences. Trying to force a change in values may lead to a situation in which the other person will satisfy you with lip service and continue to behave according to his or her values. If the difference in values represents opposite poles on a polarity, the two parties may wish to treat this as a paradox to be balanced. Each side may bring a rich perspective that, if integrated, will create a stronger partnership.

Understanding the Individual Paradox

Each of us has attributes of which we are quite proud. We also have attributes that we would like to hide. The contrast suggests an individual paradox. Susan had started a successful paper goods business based on her understanding of the market and her knowledge of how to sell. Her uncanny ability to anticipate her customers' needs allowed her to visualize the market two years in advance. Planning for tomorrow and the day after tomorrow was, however, another matter. She could not manage her employees because she did not know what should be tackled immediately. This paradox represented a significant threat to the long-term health of her business. Susan's tendency, of course, was to rely on her strength—to focus on what the business would become. In the interim, Susan's employees were frustrated by a lack of concrete direction.

As we have learned throughout this chapter, one of the key ingredients in dealing with paradox is to provide space to the shadow end. We need to understand that many of our personal weaknesses can become strengths if we focus on balancing the polarities rather than hiding from the conflict. Susan's inability to deal with day-to-day concerns could be what keeps her from being dragged into the short-term fads of the day. If she were to create a partnership with someone who shared her dream and also had the ability to successfully manage in the short term, she could maximize her strengths and maintain the direction of the business. If she were to continue to hide from this paradox, she and the company could fail.

Developing Greater Understanding of Your Individual Paradoxes

Purpose: To identify the paradoxes that exist within us

Step 1   Make a list of the adjectives that people use to describe you. This list should include the perceptions of people you like and dislike—your fans and detractors. Make a complete list. You may wish to share it with someone who knows you well.

Place the words into two columns. In the left column, write adjectives about which you feel proud. In the right column, write adjectives about which you feel less comfortable.

Step 2   Draw lines connecting the words that might be considered paradoxes. Create an individual paradox minefield, similar to the organizational paradox minefield.

Step 3   For each paradox, locate where you are on the continuum. Choose a paradox that, if you were to improve the balance, would yield the biggest benefit to you.

Step 4   Create a Polarity Map™ for the paradox you wish to pursue. For each extreme, list the words that describe the positive and negative aspects of the paradox, and place them in the appropriate box. Include what you are trying to avoid and the goal you wish to achieve.

Step 5   Create a goal statement for how you intend to balance your paradox. This statement should include the following points:
   • What you wish to move away from
   • What you want to move toward
   • By when you want to make the change
   • The impact you expect this to have
   • What you will do to make it happen

Step 6   Find a partner who will coach you in developing a plan to reach your goal. The coach should focus on helping you to understand what your paradoxes are and to accept them as critical first steps in dealing with personal paradox.

Thinking in Extremes

Psychologists know that humans tend to view themselves at the extreme end of a continuum and at the same time wish to be at the other end. The examples in Figure 6-10 are common. In reality, most people are not at either end of the polarity; they are somewhere in between.

Thinking in extremes immediately puts people into a paradoxical situation, for it indicates that they are unhappy with their current situation and perceive the other end of the continuum as impossible to achieve. If I believe that I am fat and I will never become skinny, I may never try to lose weight. It is little wonder that many overweight people only half-heartedly attempt to lose weight.

If we are successful in changing our existing paradigm of extremes, we can move beyond the accompanying emotional frus-

I am fat	————————————————	I am skinny
I am rich	————————————————	I am poor
I am successful	————————————————	I am failing
I am loved	————————————————	I am unloved

Figure 6-10: Examples of Thinking in Extremes

tration. The truth is we may never be as rich, as skinny, or as successful as we desire. Most of life happens in the middle or in the dynamic tension of the two extremes.

Many leaders are told that they overmanage their employees. Their immediate response is to move to the other end of the continuum and allow their employees complete freedom while completely abandoning their former position. Naturally, this arrangement leads to employees not receiving proper direction and feedback. When the change in behavior does not result in a positive outcome, the leader reverts to his/her previous style and again overmanages employees. From each of their perspectives, employees and managers come to see the situation as inevitable. The manager says, "See, I was right, the employees couldn't perform, so I had to go back and manage the situation." The employees say, "See, I told you my manager could not stay out of the day-to-day details. What's the use of our taking the initiative?"

Trying to live on one end of a paradox seldom works in the long term. Entrepreneurs, for example, may be criticized for being incapable of walking away from the day-to-day activities of their businesses. When they stay away from decision making, they observe that the business fails to move in the direction they desire. When they again become involved in decision making, the employees are apt to step back and let the leader run the show. Edward, whom we met in Chapter 4, is in this situation.

Rather than focus on the management of tasks, it may help to better understand the needs of the parties and develop a course of action that satisfies the needs of both. For example, entrepreneurs typically want to:

• Operate a financially successful company
• Ensure high levels of customer satisfaction with the products/services being offered by the company
• Move the business in a direction consistent with their dream

Employees typically want to:

• Work for a company that is financially sound
• Satisfy customers
• Have an impact on decisions that affect their work
• Be appreciated

The example shows that overlapping objectives of entrepreneurs and their employees will not to be immediately recognized by either party. The paradox will be experienced when the owner's dream does not match what the employees are delivering. The paradox is magnified when financial results fall short of expectations. Frustration occurs when the entrepreneur sees events unfolding and feels powerless to effect change.

The resolution, as with all paradoxes, lies in balancing the extremes. It is as if the leader must resolve two simultaneous questions:

How can the entrepreneur get the expected results?
  AND
How can employees influence how they go about their work?

If the entrepreneur has the stronger hand, he or she will conclude that employees, for fear of retribution, act only when they are told to act. Typically, employees lack a broad perspective on the organization, its environment, and its strategic goals. Lacking strategic and long-term direction, employees with the best of intentions will not achieve the entrepreneur's dream. But the entrepreneur has the resources and the knowledge to add value to issues faced by employees. The way to balance this paradox lies partly in ensuring that each party understands the expectations of the other. Rather than dictate how work should be accomplished, the entrepreneur could communicate the larger perspective, the expectations, and perhaps the practices that have succeeded in the past. The employees could be prepared to consider what should be accomplished, plan to do the work, and meet the expected timetables. The resulting contract will allow both parties space to operate and will open a channel for communication. Focusing the process on coming to agreement rather than on the specific tasks often helps everyone to deal with paradox. The exercise below encourages discussion. It should only be undertaken with the assistance of a trained facilitator.

Exercise: Understand Personal Extremes

Purpose: To understand the pole preferences we see in ourselves, to understand the pole preferences we believe about others, and to find a way to manage our extremes

Step 1   Bring together leaders and followers or peers who must work together. Ask each individual to list the paradoxes they experience in their relationships with the other people in the room. The focus here is on paradoxes, not problems. Ask each person to identify his or her most critical paradox.

Step 2   One individual shares his or her most critical paradox and the bind it puts her in. If the paradox affects another person in the room, the two parties develop a Polarity Map™ to find greater balance between them.

When Organizational, Role, and Personal Paradoxes Collide

We all dream. However, achieving one's dreams often results in unintended consequences. A high-school athlete becomes a professional athlete and then cannot handle being in the spotlight. A successful entrepreneur's hard work and dedication results in an organization she can no longer manage and control. A dedicated employee receives a hard-earned promotion, only to find that relationships with colleagues are no longer satisfying.

We are frequently exhorted to become all that we are capable of achieving. We fantasize that once we have achieved our dream, all will be well in our world. Life is paradox. Learning to balance paradoxes can be a life-long challenge.

Paradox teaches us that for every patch of sunshine there will be a patch of shadow. The silver bullet so effective in one era becomes an anchor in the next. Great leaders successfully guide their followers through to the other side of paradox. The private anguish of the leader enables the community to thrive.

When we successfully incorporate both sides of a paradox into the organization or ourselves, we become stronger. Courage, insight, and the processes outlined in this chapter may be helpful in balancing paradox. Finding others to travel with us through the experience is a precious gift.

We have now come full circle. When we are in the midst of an organizational, role, or individual crisis because what worked yesterday no longer works today, it is time to take stock, slow down the pace of our lives, and make some hard decisions. We must decide if we are going to move to a different organization, change roles, or change how we operate.

Summary

Paradox occurs when two opposites exist at the same time or in the same space. Paradoxes may be experienced at the organizational, role, or individual level.

Paradoxes cannot be solved—they must be balanced. If we pursue either end of the paradox to the neglect of the other, unintended consequences will occur.

A paradigm is a set of rules about how to perceive the world. When old paradigms conflict with a new reality, paradox may result.

A major source of organizational paradox is the division of people and their work into functions. Each functional group is needed to accomplish the mission of the organization. Problems occur whenever functions assume that they can successfully operate independently of other functions. Thus each function is likely to both help and hinder the organization's ability to succeed.

A common leadership mistake is to treat all issues as problems. A problem typically has one or more preferred solutions, that when applied, solve the problem. When we face a recurring issue, one that has "both/and" solutions, we are dealing with a paradox. Confusing a problem with a paradox is costly at all three levels: organizational, role, and individual.

Conflict is a natural aspect of organizational life. Selecting among the five conflict styles depends on such factors as your relationship with the other party, the power you have in the relationship, the importance of the issue to you, and the amount of support you require from others. Especially difficult are situations in which the values of two parties conflict.

Environment and Leadership Assessment: A Tool for Leaders and Followers

This assessment is designed to give you a perspective on leadership in your organization. It is focused around the five key challenges for leaders: redefining the map, developing followership, teaching and learning, building community, and balancing Paradox.

Respond to each statement under "As an Organization" from the perspective of what your organization is like today. For example, when responding to "When we face our competitors in the marketplace, we win the business," make your assessment from today's reality, not from what you'd like it to be.

Respond to each statement under "The Leadership" either from your perspective as the leader (if you are the leader) of the organization or organizational unit, or from your perspective as an employee evaluating the performance of your leader or leaders.

Table A-1: Environment and Leadership Assessment Tool

Please complete the following items by responding to the statements with your honest assessment of how much you agree or disagree. Use the following responses to give your answer: Strongly Disagree (SD), Disagree (D), Neutral (N), Agree (A), or Strongly Agree (SA).

As an Organization:

	SD	D	N	A	SA
1. When we face our competitors in the marketplace, we win the business.	1	2	3	4	5
2. Our ideas about this business can withstand changes in the marketplace.	1	2	3	4	5
3. It is clear where our organization needs to go to ensure long-term growth and prosperity.	1	2	3	4	5
4. Our products and services exceed customer expectations	1	2	3	4	5
5. We successfully partner with others to improve our products and services.	1	2	3	4	5
6. People challenge leadership to keep them honest and informed.	1	2	3	4	5
7. There are always plenty of volunteers to take on new challenges and critical work.	1	2	3	4	5
8. People generally exceed performance expectations.	1	2	3	4	5
9. People in our organization hold themselves to a higher standard than the work requires.	1	2	3	4	5
10. People are able to think for themselves and express their thoughts openly.	1	2	3	4	5
11. Most people in the organization understand how our business works.	1	2	3	4	5

12. People know what they need to in order to do their jobs. 1 2 3 4 5
13. We use ideas from outside the organization to improve how we do business. 1 2 3 4 5
14. We are good at learning from our successes and failures. 1 2 3 4 5
15. Managers effectively train and teach. 1 2 3 4 5
16. People work effectively together across departments. 1 2 3 4 5
17. People use our values and operating principles to guide their behavior and make decisions. 1 2 3 4 5
18. Our human resources and management information systems support our business needs. 1 2 3 4 5
19. Our organization is diverse in experience, values, perceptions, attitudes, and background. 1 2 3 4 5
20. People hold themselves and each other accountable for getting things done. 1 2 3 4 5
21. When there is change and controversy, people are still able to focus on their work. 1 2 3 4 5
22. We confront difficult issues in a timely way. 1 2 3 4 5
23. We are able to preserve teamwork while taking difficult and painful action. 1 2 3 4 5
24. We include the unpopular voices when making decisions. 1 2 3 4 5
25. We are able to effectively serve our customers while exploring and testing new possibilities and future directions. 1 2 3 4 5

Table A-1: Environment and Leadership Assessment Tool (continued)

Please complete the following items by responding to the statements with your honest assessment of how often the described behavior or conditions occur. Use the following responses to give your answer: Never (N), Seldom (SE), Sometimes (ST), Usually (U), or Always (A). To the right of the leadership questions is a blank line for evidence designed to aid in choosing a response. Use the evidence column to list concrete examples to help you choose your response.

The Leadership:	N	SE	ST	U	A	Evidence
26. Regularly connects with our customers to understand their current and future needs.	1	2	3	4	5	_____
27. Actively manages change in our organization.	1	2	3	4	5	_____
28. Follows through to ensure the development and delivery of new products and services.	1	2	3	4	5	_____
29. Understands the business in the context of our industry and market.	1	2	3	4	5	_____
30. Focuses on how we will realistically need to be different in the future.	1	2	3	4	5	_____
31. Models behaviors consistent with our purpose and values.	1	2	3	4	5	_____
32. Encourages people to lead and supports them.	1	2	3	4	5	_____
33. Regularly seeks the opinions of others before making decisions.	1	2	3	4	5	_____
34. Would be elected to lead if this were a democracy.	1	2	3	4	5	_____
35. Actively supports critical and independent thinking in the workplace.	1	2	3	4	5	_____
36. Acts on learning to change the business.	1	2	3	4	5	_____
37. Seeks candid feedback about their performance.	1	2	3	4	5	_____

38. Collects and tells success stories that illustrate how our business should work.   1 2 3 4 5 _____

39. Assists people to grow professionally through their coaching.   1 2 3 4 5 _____

40. Is sought out by employees for support and help.   1 2 3 4 5 _____

41. Consistently recognizes superior performance and addresses the needs of poor performers.   1 2 3 4 5 _____

42. Ensures that information flows to all corners of the organization.   1 2 3 4 5 _____

43. Actively develops future leaders of the organization.   1 2 3 4 5 _____

44. Brings difficult issues to the surface and ensures that they are addressed.   1 2 3 4 5 _____

45. Keeps a manageable number of important issues on the table.   1 2 3 4 5 _____

46. Constructively manages controversy over how best to achieve the organization's goals.   1 2 3 4 5 _____

47. Takes significant personal risk to resolve difficult issues.   1 2 3 4 5 _____

48. Creatively finds solutions when none are apparent.   1 2 3 4 5 _____

49. Balances what's right in the long term, with what's expedient in the short term.   1 2 3 4 5 _____

50. Effectively manages the competing interests of employees, shareholders, and other stakeholders.   1 2 3 4 5 _____

To score add the numbers for the questions and place the totals in the boxes to the right.

Challenge		Question Number	Environment	Question Number	Execution
Reframe Future	(R)	1-5		26-30	
Develop Commitment	(D)	6-10		31-35	
Teach & Learn	(T)	11-15		36-40	
Build Community	(C)	16-20		41-45	
Balance Paradox	(Px)	21-25		46-50	

Figure A-1: Leader Assessment Scoring Grid

For each leader challenge use the Environment and Execution totals as coordinates to locate it on the grid. Write in the symbol at that location. Repeat for each.

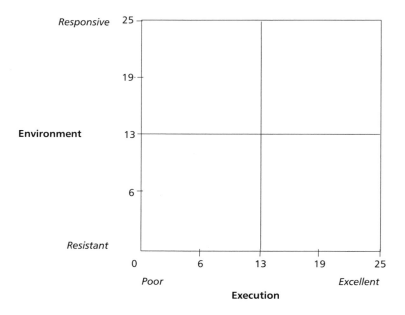

Figure A-2: Environment/Execution Grid

Interpreting the Results

As you examine your results consider the following questions and thoughts.

- Where does your execution as a leader intersect with extreme challenges to the business?
- Are you driven by urgency or by vision?
- Are you using every opportunity to communicate your passion about the business?
- Are you getting regular and reliable feedback on your performance and its impact on your reports and the rest of the organization?
- What are the areas of greatest strength and where are your weaknesses?
- Do you use your strengths to develop other leaders?
- Where do you need to build your strength and skills?
- How will you address your weaknesses?

APPENDIX B

Communicating Organizational and Team Change

Often people assume that if communication were improved, everyone would be able to work together. But what is "better communication"? What are the areas where people need to become more informed? How do we assess where an organization needs to focus?

Most leaders respond by giving people more transaction messages. Rather then helping the situation, this can actually clog the airwaves. Below is one way to categorize the kind of information that may be helpful to employees. It is applicable to large and small organizations as well as to teams and individuals.

The Approach

Table B-1 outlines the major areas where the focus can begin.

Table B-1: Communicating Change

Step	Purpose	Process	Outcome	Questions
Strategy	What do we need to do?	• Planning session • Determination of vision/mission/values/major objectives • Development of specific action plans to meet the objectives of the organization	• Approved business plan • Understanding of the big picture • Knowledge of how my work fits into the whole	• Does each team member understand the mission/vision/values/major objectives of the team? • Do people feel that they have had the appropriate level of involvement? • How was it determined what to accomplish? • Was the necessary information communicated? • Is there agreement and understanding of what needs to be accomplished? • How do we know these things?
Structure	How/where are decisions made?	• Structure meeting • Chartering process • Edict	• Organization chart • Responsibilities matrix • Decision-making process	• Are the right people making the decisions? • Is there a process for making ongoing decisions as conditions change? • Is the appropriate method(s) being used to make decisions? • Is there a forum when for people who disagree? • Are there ways to hold people accountable to ensure that performance is being achieved? • How do you know this?
Process	How will work be done?	• Process management/reengineering/quality improvement	• New/improved processes	• Are people clear about how tasks are to be accomplished?

		• Clarity about how the work will be performed • Flow charting process • Determination of process leader	• Is there the appropriate linkage between different parts of the organization? • Are the right people taking the appropriate accountability for completion of the work? • Is the team using the appropriate tools, such as flow analysis, measuring performance, and reducing tasks that add no value? • Is there an appropriate balance between productive capability and production? • How do you know this?
Roles/responsibilities	Who will do the work?	• Role clarification • Job description • Performance contracting	• Department charters • Team /individual job descriptions	• Do people know what they are supposed to do? • Was the method used to establish roles considered by team members to be appropriate? • Is the leader assured that each person understands his or her role and accepts it? • Has the clarification of roles been confirmed? • How do you know this?
Learning	What do people need to know to do the job?	• Coaching • Training programs • Autopsies • Problem-solving sessions • Systems thinking approaches	• Organizational review • Individual and team development plans	• Do the individuals have the skills to fulfill the roles? • If the skills are not present, does the individual have a person who will mentor him or her? • Is there a development plan in place? • Is there a follow-up to the development plan? • Are there opportunities for coaching/mentoring and/or training? • How do you know this?

Table B-1: Communicating Change (continued)

Step	Purpose	Process	Outcome	Questions
Systems	How do we know we accomplished the goal?	• Performance management • Financial systems • Technical systems	• Systems in place to coordinate, evaluate, and facilitate flow of information	• Do people have the appropriate information to evaluate how well they and their team are doing? • Do we have the appropriate systems and methods in place to collect the information? How do we know they are accurate? • How often is the information collected? • How do you know?
Measures	How will we evaluate effectiveness, efficiency, and competitiveness?	Develop for each process, business result (outputs), & individual/team: • Regular review • Hold people accountable	Knowledge of whether we are meeting expectations as: • An organization • A business unit • A cross-functional team • An individual	• Have we determined the most appropriate measures by which to judge our performance? • Are there process and results measures? • Does the team agree that these are the appropriate measures? • Are the measures described before the task is undertaken? • Does the team use the information to judge its performance and make the necessary changes?

Bibliography

Argyris, Chris and Schön, Donald A., *Organizational Learning: A Theory of Action Perspective*. Reading, MA: Addison-Wesley, 1978.

Barker, Joel, *Paradigms: The Business of Discovering the Future*. New York: HarperBusiness, 1992.

Beckhard, Richard and Harris, Reuben, *Managing Organization Transitions: Managing Complex Change*. Reading, MA: Addison-Wesley, 1987.

Beckhard, Richard and Pritchard, Wendy, *Changing the essence: The art of creating and leading fundamental change in organizations*. San Francisco: Jossey-Bass, 1992.

Beer, Michael, Eisenstat, R. A., and Spector, B., *The Critical Path to Corporate Renewal*. Boston: Harvard Business School Press, 1990.

Bennis, Warren and Nanus, Burt, *Leaders*. New York: Harper & Row, 1985.

Block, Peter, *Stewardship*. San Francisco: Berrett-Koehler, 1993.

Collins, James and Jerry Porras, *Built to Last: Successful Habits of Visionary Companies*. New York: HarperCollins, 1997.

Culbert, Samuel A. and McDonough, John J., *Radical Management: Power Politics and the Pursuit of Trust*. New York: The Free Press, 1985.

Dyer, William G., *Strategies for Managing Change*. Reading, MA: Addison-Wesley, 1984.

Farson, Richard, *Management of the Absurd: Paradoxes in Leadership*. New York: Touchstone, 1996.

Fletcher, Jerry and Kelle, Olwyler, *Paradoxical Thinking: How to Profit from Your Contradictions*. San Francisco: Berett-Koehler, 1997.

Goleman, Daniel, *Emotional Intelligence*. New York: Bantam, 1995.

Gozdz, Kasimierz, *Community Building*. San Francisco: New Leaders Press, 1995.

Hamel, Gary and C. K. Prahalad, *Competing for the Future*. Boston: Harvard Business School Press, 1994.

Handy, Charles, *The Hungry Spirit, Beyond Capitalism: A Quest for Purpose in the Modern World.* New York: Broadway Books, 1998.

Handy, Charles, *The Age of Unreason.* Boston: Harvard Business School Press, 1989.

Hesselbein, Frances, Goldsmith, Marshall, Bechard, Richard, and Schubert, Richard, *The Community of the Future.* San Francisco: Jossey-Bass, 1998.

Jacobson, Ralph, "The real work of teams." *Human Systems Management* 15 (1996): 71–78.

Johnson, Barry, *Polarity Management: Identifying and Managing Unresolvable Problems.* Amherst, MA: HRD Press, 1996.

Kaplan, Robert and Norton, David, *The Balanced Scorecard.* Boston: Harvard Business School Press, 1996.

Katzenbach and the RCL Team, *Real Change Leaders.* New York: Random House, 1995.

Kelley, Robert, *The Power of Followership.* New York: Currency Books, 1992.

Land, George and Beth Jarman, *Breakpoint and Beyond: Mastering the Future Today.* New York: HarperBusiness, 1992.

Lewis, Jordan, *Partnerships for Profit: Structuring and Managing Strategic Alliances.* New York: The Free Press, 1990.

O'Toole, James, *Leading Change: Overcoming the Ideology of Comfort and the Tyranny of Custom.* San Francisco: Jossey-Bass, 1995.

Pascale, Richard T., *Managing on the Edge.* New York: Simon and Schuster, 1990.

Porter, Michael, *Competitve Advantage.* New York: The Free Press, 1985.

Price Waterhouse Change Team, *The Paradox Principles: How High-Performance Companies Manage Chaos, Complexity, and Contradiction to Achieve Superior Results.* Chicago: Irwin, 1996.

Quinn, Robert, *Beyond Rational Management: Mastering the Paradoxes and Competing Demands of High Performance.* San Francisco: Jossey-Bass, 1988.

Quinn, Robert, Faermannn, Sue, Thompson, Michael, and McGrath, Mitch, *Becoming a Master Manager, a Competency Framework.* New York: John Wiley & Sons, 1995.

Schwartz, Peter, *The Art of the Long View: Planning the Future in an Uncertain World.* New York: Doubleday, 1991.

Seiling, Jane Galloway, *The Membership Organization.* Palo Alto, CA: Davies-Black Publishing, 1997.

Senge, Peter, Roberts, Charlotte, Ross, Richard, Smith, Byron, and Kleiner, Art, *Fifth Discipline Handbook.* New York: Doubleday, 1994.

Senge, Peter, *The Fifth Discipline: The Art and Practice of the Learning Organization*. New York: Doubleday, 1990.

Shaffer, Carolyn R. and Anundsen, Kristin, *Creating Community Anywhere*. New York: Tarcher/Putnum, 1993.

Shaw, Gordon, Brown, Robert, and Bromiley, Philip, "Strategic Stories: How 3M is Rewriting Business Planning." *Harvard Business Review*, May-June 1998.

Stacey, Ralph, *Managing the Unknowable: Strategic Boundaries Between Order and Chaos in Organizations*, San Francisco: Jossey-Bass, 1992.

Sullivan, Gordon and Harper, Michael, *Hope Is Not a Method*. New York: Random House, 1996.

Tichy, Noel, *The Leadership Engine*. New York: HarperBusiness, 1997.

Van Der Heijden, Kees, *Scenarios: The Art of Strategic Conversation*. West Sussex, England: John Wiley and Sons, 1997.

Wills, Garry, *Certain Trumpets: The Nature of Leadership*. New York: Simon and Schuster, 1994.

Index

Butterworth-Heinemann Business Books . . . for Transforming Business

Corporate DNA: Learning from Life,
  Ken Baskin, 0-7506-9844-6

Cultivating Common Ground: Releasing the Power of Relationships at Work,
  Daniel S. Hanson, 0-7506-9832-2

Flight of the Phoenix: Soaring to Success in the 21st Century,
  John Whiteside and Sandra Egli, 0-7506-9798-9

Getting a Grip on Tomorrow: Your Guide to Survival and Success in the Changed World of Work,
  Mike Johnson, 0-7506-9758-X

Innovation Strategy for the Knowledge Economy: The Ken *Awakening,*
  Debra M. Amidon, 0-7506-9841-1

Innovation Through Intuition: The Hidden Intelligence,
  Sandra Weintraub, 0-7506-9937-X

The Intelligence Advantage: Organizing for Complexity,
  Michael D. McMaster, 0-7506-9792-X

Intuitive Imagery: A Resource at Work,
  John B. Pehrson and Susan E. Mehrtens, 0-7506-9805-5

The Knowledge Evolution: Expanding Organizational Intelligence,
  Verna Allee, 0-7506-9842-X

Large Scale Organizational Change: An Executive's Guide,
  Christopher Laszlo and Jean-Francois Laugel, 0-7506-7230-7

Leadership in a Challenging World: A Sacred Journey,
  Barbara Shipka, 0-7506-9750-4

Leading Consciously: A Pilgrimage Toward Self Mastery,
  Debashis Chatterjee, 0-7506-9864-0

Leading from the Heart: Choosing Courage over Fear in the Workplace,
  Kay Gilley, 0-7506-9835-7

Learning to Read the Signs: Reclaiming Pragmatism in Business,
F. Byron Nahser, 0-7506-9901-9

Leveraging People and Profit: The Hard Work of Soft Management,
Bernard A. Nagle and Perry Pascarella, 0-7506-9961-2

Marketing Plans That Work: Targeting Growth and Profitability,
Malcolm H.B. McDonald and Warren J. Keegan, 0-7506-9828-4

A Place to Shine: Emerging from the Shadows at Work,
Daniel S. Hanson, 0-7506-9738-5

Power Partnering: A Strategy for Business Excellence in the 21st Century,
Sean Gadman, 0-7506-9809-8

Putting Emotional Intelligence to Work: Successful Leadership Is More Than IQ,
David Ryback, 0-7506-9956-6

Resources for the Knowledge-Based Economy Series
The Knowledge Economy,
Dale Neef, 0-7506-9936-1
Knowledge Management and Organizational Design,
Paul S. Myers, 0-7506-9749-0
Knowledge Management Tools,
Rudy L. Ruggles, III, 0-7506-9849-7
Knowledge in Organizations,
Laurence Prusak, 0-7506-9718-0
The Strategic Management of Intellectual Capital,
David A. Klein, 0-7506-9850-0
Knowledge, Groupware and the Internet,
David Smith, 0-7506-7111-4
Knowledge and Social Capital,
Eric Lesser, 0-7506-7222-6
Strategic Learning in a Knowledge Economy,
Robert Cross, and Sam Israelit, 0-7506-7223-4

The Rhythm of Business: The Key to Building and Running Successful Companies,
Jeffrey C. Shuman, 0-7506-9991-4

Setting the PACE® in Product Development: A Guide to Product and Cycle-Time Excellence,
    Michael E. McGrath, 0-7506-9789-X

Time to Take Control: The Impact of Change on Corporate Computer Systems,
    Tony Johnson, 0-7506-9863-2

The Transformation of Management,
    Mike Davidson, 0-7506-9814-4

Unleashing Intellectual Capital,
    Charles Ehin, 0-7506-7246-3

What Is the Emperor Wearing? Truth-Telling in Business Relationships,
    Laurie Weiss, 0-7506-9872-1

Who We Could Be at Work, Revised Edition,
    Margaret A. Lulic, 0-7506-9739-3

Working from Your Core: Personal and Corporate Wisdom in a World of Change,
    Sharon Seivert, 0-7506-9931-0

To purchase any Butterworth-Heinemann title, please visit your local bookstore or call 1-800-366-2665.